# HILLARY
# RODHAM
# CLINTON

# HILLARY RODHAM CLINTON

## A FIRST LADY FOR OUR TIME

### DONNIE RADCLIFFE

WARNER BOOKS

A Time Warner Company

E
887
.C55
R33
1993

To my husband, Bob, who never doubted
where my place was, and
to all women who
are looking for theirs.

Warner Books, Inc., 1271 Avenue of the Americas,
New York, NY 10020

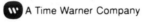 A Time Warner Company

Printed in the United States of America
First Printing: September 1993
10   9   8   7   6   5   4   3   2   1

Library of Congress Cataloging-in-Publication Data

Radcliffe, Donnie.
    Hillary Rodham Clinton : a first lady for our time / Donnie
Radcliffe.
        p.   cm.
    Includes index.
    ISBN 0-446-51766-6
    1. Clinton, Hillary Rodham.   2. Clinton, Bill, 1946–
3. Presidents—United States—Wives—Biography.   I. Title.
E887.C55R33    1993
973.929'092—dc20
[B]                                                              92-51038
                                                                      CIP

*Book design by H. Roberts*

# Acknowledgments

EVERY WORD, PHRASE, sentence, paragraph and page
was possible because of someone among the nearly one
hundred fifty people I talked to in the process of writing
this book. I especially want to thank Hillary Rodham
Clinton, whom I interviewed on two occasions, once
during the 1992 campaign and once at the end of
President Clinton's first one hundred days in office. I
am extremely grateful to several members of her staff,
including Lisa Caputo, Melanne Verveer, Maggie Williams and Neel Lattimore.

Along the way, there were Hillary Rodham Clinton's childhood friends, church mentors and teachers
in Park Ridge, Illinois; her fellow students and professors at Wellesley College and Yale Law School; her

associates and friends on the Impeachment Inquiry Staff of the House Judiciary Committee; her friends, faculty associates and students at the University of Arkansas and its law school; her legal colleagues, associates and friends throughout Arkansas; her co-workers in various political campaigns and others who don't necessarily fit neatly into any category. I have tried to mention as many as possible by name. Those I don't mention were important conduits to information I was seeking.

I especially want to mention those who went the extra mile to lend additional behind-the-scenes assistance and support by digging into their memories, photo albums, scrapbooks, little black books, files and archives. Particularly helpful were Otto Kohler, Ellen Press Murdoch, Ernest "Rick" Ricketts, Diane Blair, Ann Henry, the Reverend Don Jones, Stephen London, the Reverend H. Paul Santmire, Alan Schechter, John Bibby, Gary Speed, Maya Alleruzzo, Fred Altshuler, Sam Donaldson, Jan Smith, Robert Barnett, Karen Larsen, Kathy Imber, Marlan Davis, Kenneth Reese, Laverne Steffens, the Reverend Guy Morrison, Madeleine Dubek, Anne Gasior, Laurel Stavis, Wilma R. Slaight, Christina Rambeau, Jean Berry, Martin W. G. King, Margaret Summers, Peggy Lampl, Lee Edel, Nancy Williams, David Gearhart, Malcolm McNair, Kenneth Reese, Barbara Turner, Leon Osgood, Baytop Fitzhugh III, John Deardourff, Elisabeth Griffith, Nancy Beardsley, the Reverend William T. Coleman III, Donald Pogue, Susan Bucknell, Brenda Blagg, Tom Hamburger, Marian Wright Edelman, Stella Ogata, Lynn Bowersox, Bequita Gray, Betty Bumpers, Skip Rutherford, Dagmar Hamilton, Woody Bassett,

Van Gearhart, Luther Rawls Williams, Gerald Baker, Betsey Wright, David Matthews, Edwin J. Feulner, Joan Campbell, Judge Thomas Butt, Robert Leflar, Sharon Souther, Claudia Polley, Ann Laeuchli, Catherine Inno, Harriett Jansma, Craig Smith, Kiki Moore, Kelly Lee, Ann Mantle and many others.

In the absence of footnotes, I tried to identify or credit writers and their publications within the body of the text. Of invaluable assistance was my longtime friend and colleague Marian Burros, writing in both *The New York Times* and *Family Circle*. I particularly want to mention my fellow reporters at *The Washington Post*, Martha Sherrill, Lloyd Grove, David Maraniss and Roxanne Roberts. I am grateful to many others at the *Post* for their interest and encouragement, including Sarah Booth Conroy, Lou Cannon, Karen Mason Marrero, Bobbye Pratt, Elizabeth Kastor, Jura Koncius, Patsy Rogers, Ann Mariano, Brenda Caggiano and Sandy Flickner.

I especially wish to thank Style Editor Mary Hadar, Executive Editor Leonard Downie and Managing Editor Robert Kaiser, for granting me a leave of absence and then allowing me to extend it.

The genealogical research was the highly professional detective work of Andrew Naprawa, who came to me through the auspices of Toni Murray and Matthew Lesko of Information USA, Inc. I also want to thank Cecile Belisle Champagne for her sleuthing in Pennsylvania.

Probably no one was more enthusiastic about the Hillary story than my "legman" in Scranton, Pennsylvania, Guy Rodney, a longtime friend, admirer and neighbor of Hillary's grandfather. Guy voluntarily came out of retirement and into my heart.

Many, many friends gave me moral support and encouragement and in many instances put up with my neglect but did not abandon me. Notable among them were Carl Sferrazza Anthony, author of the two-volume *First Ladies*, Barbara Feinman, Ann Sandler, Jane McCreary, Whitney Cole, Jean and Sam Iker, Molly Kellogg, Jan DuPlain, John and Deborah Fialka, Pat Blair, Shahin Bagheri, Linda Canturk, Claire and Maclay Burt, Ed DeFontaine, Buzz Cranston, Sharon King, Gail Fleischman, Jennifer Nunes, Steve Raymer, Mary Hoyt, Jennifer Gallagher, Bob and June Trayhern.

I appreciate the patience of Joann Davis, Jean-Marie Lemense and others at Warner Books. I am grateful to my agent and friend Gail Ross, who has always been there when I needed her.

To those I may have neglected to name, I sincerely apologize. Believe me, I needed you, too.

And, finally, I am indebted to two people in particular, Brian Kelly and Robin Groom, both valued colleagues of mine at *The Washington Post* whose unflagging encouragement, guidance and help—tangible and intangible—kept me on the straight and narrow. They don't come any better in this word business. To them and to my own family, I can only quote Shakespeare, who said it all:

> I can no other answer make but thanks,
> And thanks,
> And ever thanks.

# Contents

Preface                                              xiii

1. *Victory!*                                           1
2. *The Making of a Politician*                        21
3. *An Activist in the Making*                          53
4. *Coming of Age at Yale*                              85
5. *From Front Row to Center Stage*                    109
6. *A Verdict of Love*                                 131
7. *Trials and Errors*                                 153
8. *Mistaken Identity*                                 177
9. *Making Her Mark*                                   199
10. *They Shoot Candidates' Wives, Don't They?*        223
11. *A Place of Her Own*                               239

Index                                                 263

# Hugh E. Rodham

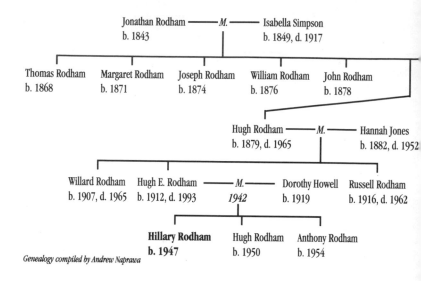

Jonathan Rodham — *M.* — Isabella Simpson
b. 1843           b. 1849, d. 1917

Thomas Rodham   Margaret Rodham   Joseph Rodham   William Rodham   John Rodham
b. 1868      b. 1871      b. 1874      b. 1876      b. 1878

Hugh Rodham — *M.* — Hannah Jones
b. 1879, d. 1965      b. 1882, d. 1952

Willard Rodham   Hugh E. Rodham — *M.* — Dorothy Howell   Russell Rodham
b. 1907, d. 1965   b. 1912, d. 1993   *1942*   b. 1919      b. 1916, d. 1962

**Hillary Rodham**   Hugh Rodham   Anthony Rodham
**b. 1947**      b. 1950      b. 1954

*Genealogy compiled by Andrew Naprawa*

---

# Dorothy Howell Rodham

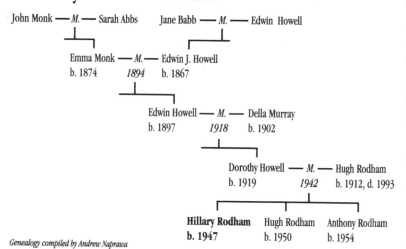

John Monk — *M.* — Sarah Abbs     Jane Babb — *M.* — Edwin Howell

Emma Monk — *M.* — Edwin J. Howell
b. 1874   *1894*   b. 1867

Edwin Howell — *M.* — Della Murray
b. 1897   *1918*   b. 1902

Dorothy Howell — *M.* — Hugh Rodham
b. 1919      *1942*   b. 1912, d. 1993

**Hillary Rodham**   Hugh Rodham   Anthony Rodham
**b. 1947**      b. 1950      b. 1954

*Genealogy compiled by Andrew Naprawa*

Elizabeth Rodham
b. 1881

Robert Rodham
b. 1883

Wade Rodham
b. 1885

Ethel Rodham
b. 1888

George Rodham
b. 1889

# Preface

THE STORY OF Hillary Rodham Clinton is the story of so many millions of Americans whose immigrant ancestors, desperate for change and a chance, left the Old Country for a land across the Atlantic promising opportunity and hope.

In the one hundred years beginning 1830, some thirty-two million men, women and children fled famine, poverty and oppressive governments in what would become the biggest mass movement in mankind's recorded history. England, too, where it had all started two centuries earlier, was in the grip of hard times, and as much as anywhere Northumberland, just below the Scottish border, and Wales, far to the southwest—both regions famous and notorious for their coal mines. Escaping the tyranny of both factory and mine was the hope that propelled many a young man onto a ship to America.

Such a man was Hillary's great-grandfather, Jonathan Rodham, born of people who knew only too well the dangers and despair of the coal pits in the small mining villages of Northumberland and County Durham around Newcastle. And so, too, was William Jones, believed to have been another great-grandfather, who turned his back on the mines of South Wales.

Both men were nearly the same age—Jonathan Rodham, thirty-eight, William Jones, thirty-seven—when they left for the New World at almost the same time, Jones in 1879, Rodham in 1881. And both found their way to Scranton, Pennsylvania, offering a hauntingly familiar life of factories and coal fields.

For Jonathan, the decision was made to go alone and send for his family once he found work. Isabelle Simpson Rodham, then thirty-three, and their seven children (two others had died earlier), joined him in 1882. By 1900, United States Census records show that Jonathan was a policeman in Scranton (by 1910, he was a florist) and his and Isabelle's family had grown to eleven children, nine living at home.

Among them was Hillary's grandfather Hugh Rodham, identified with three of his brothers by that turn-of-the-century census as laborers in an icehouse, a coal mine, a machine shop and in Hugh's case, a lace factory. Hugh, twenty-one that year, already had been working much of his life; he went with the Scranton Lace Works Company when he was thirteen.

Hillary's paternal grandmother, Hannah Jones,

was born in Scranton in 1882, three years after William and his wife, Mary Griffiths Jones, then thirty-two, left South Wales to begin their lives anew. The formal educations of many young women of that era often were cut short by their family's need for another bread-winner. Whether Hannah was among them is unclear, but according to the 1900 census she was a working woman at the age of eighteen—a winder in a Scranton silk mill. Two years later, she married Hugh Rodham and there are those in Scranton who remember that the name she preferred to be known by was Hannah Jones Rodham. The first of her three sons, Willard, was born in 1907. Hugh's namesake, Hillary's father, was born in 1912, followed four years later by Russell.

In Scranton, the Rodhams remained faithful to John Wesley's Methodist teachings that had sustained their Welsh and English ancestors. In England, children were expected to go to church three times a day. "We had no choice," Patricia Rodham Clayton, living in a small village near Newcastle and quite possibly a distant cousin of Hillary's father, told me in an interview.

Hardworking and thrifty, the Rodhams were typical of families who provided the heart and soul of a brash new nation. Opportunity was there for those who seized it and one who did was young Hugh Rodham, setting off from Scranton in the throes of the Depression to make his fortune elsewhere.

There is evidence that he intended to return; in 1937 he and a young Scranton woman took out a marriage license. That it was never used, perhaps, was because that was also the year he met a pretty young woman, seven years his junior, in another lace factory, this one in Chicago.

She was Hillary's mother, Dorothy Howell, whose own forebears had come from England and Canada around the same time as the Rodhams and the Joneses. Like Hillary, Dorothy was born in Chicago. Unlike Hillary, whose story begins on the city's middle-class North Side, Dorothy's began on the South Side in a working-class neighborhood.

The 1920 census shows that Dorothy, born in June 1919, lived with her parents Edwin Howell, twenty-one, and Della Murray Howell, seventeen, in a building on South Michigan Avenue near East 30th Street, among neighbors working as janitors, housekeepers, servants and clerks. Edwin's occupation was listed as a fireman for the city. He and Della had been married by a Baptist minister in June 1918, with the consent of Della's mother.

Little is known about Della Murray other than, according to the 1920 census, she was born in Illinois, her father was born in Canada and her mother in Michigan, and that, whatever the reasons, Della had been deprived of a basic education. Her husband's family, on the other hand, could trace its roots to England and Canada.

Hillary's maternal grandfather Edwin was the only child of Edwin John Howell and Emma Josephine Monk of Elgin, Illinois. This Edwin—Hillary's third great-grandfather and a machinist in an Elgin watch factory—was born in England in 1867 to Jane Babb Howell and Edwin Howell and emigrated to the United States in 1887.

Hillary's great-grandmother Emma Monk Howell was two years old when she and her parents emigrated to the United States in 1876. According to the 1910 census, Emma's father, John Monk (Hillary's great-great-grandfather), had been born in New York State, while her mother, Sarah Abbs Monk, was born in England.

Hillary's story is far from complete but genealogists, searching for ancestors of Jonathan Rodham, narrowed the field in the spring of 1993 to yet another Jonathan, born in 1779. The Rodham name—sometimes spelled Roddam—is big around the once-thriving coal mining region of Northumberland. More than a few Rodhams began leafing through family Bibles, albums and scrapbooks looking for links to America's new First Lady.

Reporter Moira Holden of the *Newcastle Chronicle & Journal* remembers the breakthrough as an anonymous tip that eventually led to Brian Boggon, a County Durham accountant, who shared with Hillary a 1779 Jonathan as their common ancestor. That Jonathan and Ann Parkinson, born in 1786, were married in 1805 and had eight children, including Joseph, born 1817. Among Joseph and Elizabeth Scurfield Rodham's progeny would be the emigrant Jonathan. By 1881, he and his wife, Isabella, were living in Oxhill with their seven children when he probably came across a newspaper advertisement promising the good life with pay to match in the coal mines around Scranton, Pennsylvania.

There is a little milk jug inscribed with the name Rodham that sits in a place of honor at the Beemish

Open Air Museum near Oxhill. The inscription on it might have been composed in 1993 for another Rodham instead of in 1827 when it was given to Patricia Rodham Clayton's great-great-grandparents as a wedding gift:

A little health, a little wealth, a little house with freedom,

And at the end a little friend, with little cause to need him.

Donnie Radcliffe
St. Leonard's Creek, Maryland
May 1993

# 1

# *Victory!*

*"You don't spend two or three days at a national political convention beating up on someone unless you're scared."*

SHE WAS THINKING about Richard Nixon, and also about Chelsea's cat.

Sitting in a hotel room in Cleveland only hours before her husband was to be elected president of the United States and she to become, arguably, the most powerful woman in the country, Hillary Rodham Clinton thought of the man who, as much as anyone, had started it all.

Richard Milhous Nixon, that glowering phenomenon of American politics, had aroused a generation of reformers, goading it with his vision of a government—and a society—that was arrogant, compassionless and unwilling to yield power. Few had been aroused more thoroughly than Hillary—and few had found such thorough vindication. Just at the moment she was helping Congress draft the rules to impeach him, Nixon had resigned from office.

Then, with bizarre irony, he had returned in February 1992 to taunt her with his sly prediction that her independence would hurt her husband's political prospects. This time his words had aroused another group—fellow conservatives who sought to turn Hillary into the issue of the day. Could it be that not once but twice in her life she would be given the satisfaction of having the final word on Richard Nixon?

Her daughter Chelsea's cat, too, was something of a symbol. Socks, the furry black-and-white stray who made Chelsea and her and Bill feel better (even if she and Bill were allergic to him), was a connection to a very different life from the one that featured the likes of Richard Nixon. Cautiously, she had begun to think about the White House and how she would give her twelve-year-old the chance to have her own life and be able to grow up as normally as possible.

That was what she was going to be focused on, she said that afternoon in Cleveland, if she woke up the day after the election and Bill had won. Socks would be part of it. She wondered, Would he be the first First Cat since Amy Carter's? A Secret Service agent had told them there were mice and rats in the White House. Could that possibly be true? Did Barbara Bush really find a rat in the swimming pool? Maybe it was because there were no cats. Hey, this was even a political plus! Cat lovers would feel enfranchised again.

"Exit poll," she deadpanned, playing the election day poll-taker. "Did you vote for the Clintons because they have a cat?"

The potential was mind-boggling.

"I love it!" Hillary Rodham Clinton cried, convulsed by a genuine moment of absurd humor. "Oh, God, I love it!"

For more than a year she had been doing this, taking the media on personally—and carefully—conducted tours of her life, times and psyche. Sometimes the tours were conducted in limousines, sometimes in airplanes, sometimes in buses. And sometimes, like this one, in a hotel room between campaign appearances when she was just passing through town. A pit stop, in a sense, allowing her to call home to Chelsea, touch up her makeup, see in private an old friend— like the one now sitting quietly across the room watching and listening with undisguised fascination—and check in with Clinton-Gore headquarters in Little Rock. And even grab a bite, like those giant strawberries sent up by the hotel management with a welcoming basket of fruit.

People could say what they wanted about Hillary's "makeover," but from across the coffee table in that decorator-contrived hotel setting of intimacy, it was only too apparent that there had been a lot to work with: good bone structure, good teeth, good skin. Coupled with the direct gaze of her blue eyes and her blonded hair, the effect of the gold earrings matching the gold buttons on her bright red blazer and the black turtleneck sweater lending just the right touch of smart casualness, was that of a serious, earnest woman who, surprisingly perhaps, also enjoyed a roaring good laugh.

Not too many hours would go by before she would be passing through Cleveland again, then it would be with Bill stopping at the airport in a mad flyaround that would cover nearly five thousand miles and barnstorm fourteen cities before finally touching down in Little Rock to vote for him as the next president.

Right now, though, she tried not to think about winning—or at least not think about it very much—partly because it wouldn't play well with the message of the day and partly because it was just bad luck.

"It's like a no-hit game," she said, no offhand quip from a onetime ace shortstop who, at age nine, could quote box scores and other statistics with the best of baseball's fanatics. In the late innings, with a few batters left, the pitcher can't afford to lose his concentration for even a moment.

And what a game it had been. The name-calling alone—Lady Macbeth of Little Rock, Winnie Mandela of American Politics, the Smiling Barracuda, That Dowdy Feminazi—had hit a new low in the trashing of a candidate's wife. But now, from the safety of Bill Clinton's ten-point lead in the polls, she could look back at the culmination of that vitriol—the calculated and relentless Hillary bashing at the Republican National Convention in Houston during the dog days of August—with a measure of philosophical pride.

"At first I was really surprised," she said. "I couldn't understand what was going on. And I was hurt a little bit because, I thought, 'Why would they spend their time at this convention going after me and misrepresenting things that I had said and worked on?'

"And then I said to myself, 'Well, obviously they're scared.' You don't spend two or three days at a national political convention beating up on someone unless you're scared." In a kind of "backhanded way," she had been complimented.

Which probably wasn't at all what Richard Nixon had had in mind ten months earlier when in his Grand Old Politician guise he had some things to say about the Clinton campaign's use of Hillary Clinton. "If the wife comes through as being too strong and too intelligent," Nixon remarked, "it makes the husband look like a wimp." And taking that a little further, according to *The New York Times*, Nixon said voters tended to agree with Cardinal de Richelieu's comment that "Intellect in a woman is unbecoming."

It had said volumes about where Richard Nixon thought most women's places were. Years before, he had elevated his mother to sainthood, his last most worshipful public reaffirmation of Hannah Nixon's place in heaven during his rambling farewell in 1974. And Teddy Roosevelt's "saintly" young first wife came in for an equally emotional mention that day. But his good wife, Pat, of the "Good Republican cloth coat"? Nary a word. Who among us at the White House that August morning could ever forget her stricken, tear-stained face as she accompanied him across the White House lawn to her own place? Measured against Nixon's standards, Pat had seemed the perfect wife. Better still, the perfect First Lady, just as Barbara Bush, in 1992, had carried on that tradition—in

Nixon's words—"as a model of a wife who has her own opinions without upstaging her husband."

Now came his practical caution to would-be wimps—not just those running for president. It couldn't have come from a guy so many baby-boomers loved to hate more. Or who had done more in shaping the life, times and psyche of one particular baby-boomer. This was the man who as president-elect in 1968 promised Lyndon Johnson to "stay the course" in Vietnam even as three hundred GIs were dying every day (and another thirteen thousand would die before he left office). Whose paranoia about rebellious and coddled college students would eventually lead to a siege mentality of secret investigations and wiretaps and White House "plumbers." Who, in one emotional outburst, managed to divide Hillary's generation of baby-boomers into cowardly bums and brave patriots. Whose I-told-you-so statement about "inviting tragedy when dissent turns to violence" after four Kent State students were shot to death and eleven others wounded by the Ohio National Guard contained not a single note of compassion for the victims or their survivors. ("My child was not a bum," said one dead girl's father.)

The list seemed to have no ending.

A generation later, *"out of the blue,"* Hillary said, the emphasis hers, Richard Nixon was back in her life attacking her. "I remember reading that, thinking to myself, 'Now, this man never does anything without a purpose. Why is he attacking me?'"

Her answer?

"Well, I thought maybe it's because he never

forgets anything—I was on the impeachment staff. But also," and here it is, an astute political analyst analyzing the Astute Political Analyst, "maybe he knew before others knew, that there was a lot going on under the surface of this country, and people were anxious for change."

Hillary's conclusion, valid or not, was that Richard Nixon "was launching a preemptive attack to try and in some way to denigrate my husband because he's unafraid of smart and intelligent women and really believes that women ought to have opportunities to serve."

But far more meaningful than her personal vilification in this quadrennial war of mudslinging had been the intensity of the debate Hillary knew was raging in newsrooms, in law firms, on factory floors and in homes about women's roles and responsibilities.

There had always been talented, energetic, effective, hardworking women—like her mother, the secretary, and Bill's mother, the nurse, fifty years earlier. They and the schoolteachers, the salesclerks, the librarians and the waitresses had carried the load of women in the work force for years, though, more often than not, without any thought to careers or their effect on society but more to the fundamental need to support themselves and their families in a closed, man's world. Only in the last twenty years—significantly, in professions where public policy affecting people's lives was being formed and were traditionally dominated by men—had the number of women working become a critical and irrefutable fact of life.

What had amazed Hillary, in those months on

the campaign trail, had been all the women who turned out for her. Not just her contemporaries, which she might have expected, but those of Dorothy Rodham and Virginia Clinton Kelley, of twelve-year-old Chelsea Victoria Clinton and her friends and others in between and beyond. They brought their babies, their daughters, their mothers and their grandmothers and held up signs with all kinds of messages about their own lives to show that they could identify with her. One sign in particular had touched her: "Stay-at-Home Moms for Hillary—I Work, Too." It was part of what Bill and Hillary Clinton had been trying to say, that this whole generational question shouldn't be exclusive; it should be inclusive.

That the debate had reached this level, and that it had been Richard Nixon who set it off, was her vindication for living her life "the way I think is right for me and my family and that's what I've always done. That's what I'll always do. That's what I want every woman to do, make choices that are right for her."

Which is why having all this occur at the presidential level was significant. It hadn't occurred there before, she believed, because, in part, "we haven't had people contending for the presidency who were born after World War II, who were really part of this change in its most widespread way." There was a "symbolic importance" to this husband-wife, man-woman, dual-career drama being acted out on the presidential level that had captured the imagination and interest of so many people. There were other issues, of course, the perilous state of the economy being the most significant, but there were times when the rhetoric of the campaign might have made one ponder if this was not a national referendum on the role of women in America.

At one point, with cracks about Hillary coming even from the incumbent, Bill Clinton had wondered aloud whether "George Bush was running for First Lady."

The whole flyaround had worked so much better than anyone ever imagined. Thousands had waited at airports in Cleveland, in Fort Worth, in Albuquerque, in Denver—many standing there in the cold and late into the night, to cheer Bill and Hillary Clinton on the final leg of their flight home to Arkansas. "The image of his resilience, his fighting for change, working until the last minute, is the image he wants to leave the country with," *Time* quoted Hillary as saying during the trip.

Between airports, Hillary and Bill had reclined in front seats—he next to the window—accorded some privacy by a blue sliding curtain. Bill—or someone—had adorned the crimson, fabric-covered bulkhead wall with campaign buttons. Beneath their feet, the floor was strewn with stuffed animals, mindful of a daughter's bedroom—or was it a long-ago college dorm? Mere hours now away from the opening of election booths across the country, Hillary allowed herself the luxury of talking about victory. "I've always been certain Bill was going to win," said this veteran of Goldwater, McCarthy, Kennedy, McGovern, Carter, Mondale and Dukakis campaigns—not just winning ones as most of Bill's had been. "I know enough about failed campaigns to recognize the averted eyes and the missed handshakes."

When their plane touched down in Little Rock that splendid fall election day morn, there was Chelsea with all the loyalists who had believed in change. Bill teased as they flocked around him that he wouldn't be staying long because he still had three more As— Arizona, Alabama and Alaska—to go. It was the same mock flight attendant spiel he had delivered on the plane that, for one awful instant, the all but brain-dead media, after forty-eight hours in the air, almost had believed. Now, on the ground for good, Bill and Hillary and all the others who had made the long night's journey into this day were deliriously happy. It wasn't just tomorrow they were thinking about.

They were thinking about winning.

By two in the afternoon, the numbers were coming in and Skip Rutherford, special assistant to campaign manager David Wilhelm, knew that his friend was going to be president of the United States. Working through his emotions on a solitary walk around downtown Little Rock, his thoughts drifted to the time in May 1991 when he and Hillary sat together at the ballpark watching their daughters play softball.

"She kept talking about how someone had to step forward and offer a new generation of leadership, a new approach, a different kind of Democrat, a change in the way things needed to be done. And that we had to find the right person. I looked over and said, 'Well, I know who that person is.' And she said, 'Well, we'll see.'"

And then there was the Saturday morning two

months later when Rutherford was taking another walk and Craig Smith, a Clinton aide, drove up and told him to get in the car because the governor wanted to "visit" with him. Unshaved and unprepared for socializing, Rutherford reluctantly climbed in the car to be driven to the Governor's Mansion where he and Smith joined Bill, Hillary and Bruce Lindsey, Bill's law partner for one brief period and a close political confidant. Standing around in the kitchen, cups of coffee in hand, "there were just a lot of what-ifs" about running for president, Rutherford remembered. "We played out various scenarios, talked about who might run, who might not run, what would happen if so-and-so runs. I don't remember anybody asking questions as much as I remember an open, free, constructive, no-holds-barred dialogue" of the type the Clintons would hold often during the next two months with various participants. "If there was ever a description of a kitchen cabinet," Rutherford said, "this was it." Later, when he returned home and was shaving, his wife walked in. "I believe Bill Clinton is going to run for president of the United States," he said. Could he win? she asked. "Sure," he said.

What Rutherford knew early on election day, the television networks would not announce for another eight hours. They had agreed not to project the exit poll data of any state until a majority of the state's precincts had closed. Little Rock had quickly turned into a carnival of expectations, bulging with people, streets impassable, hotels impenetrable. Election returns rolled endlessly across a huge outdoor television screen. People munched fried catfish and barbecue sandwiches, lost their kids, nuzzled their babies, cheered the good guys, booed the bad and in between took a few nips to stoke the inner fires. This was no longer some backwater. This was the center of the universe. You didn't have to be Arkansan to recognize the enormity of what was happening.

By nightfall, tens of thousands of Clinton supporters, indifferent to the cold, had congealed into a solid exultant mass of humanity pushing their way into history outside the Old Statehouse. There was no end of the pride they felt in this Arkansas traveler of theirs, whose journey had taken three times as long as Odysseus's, surely every bit the warrior that long-ago Greek had been. Later, Rutherford stood at the back of that crowd. What was he doing "back here" somebody wondered, noting his array of impressive campaign credentials, which surely would have admitted him to the inner sanctum. "That's the beauty of this election," Rutherford replied, caught up in the euphoria, "from this night on there won't be any 'back here' anymore."

Among those tens of thousands who came out of a sense of regional pride or just plain curiosity, there were certainly thousands who came from a very personal sense of pride and even involvement with the lives of Bill and Hillary Clinton. And though this was Bill's home state and only Hillary's adopted one, she was well supported by familiar faces from her past and present: friends and family came from her hometown of Park Ridge, Illinois; college chums from Wellesley and Yale, some of whom would play a role in the new government; political pros she'd met on the various

high-level campaigns she'd worked since Eugene Mc-
Carthy's quixotic run for the presidency in 1968; distinguished members of the Arkansas bar who'd worked
with her on high-paying corporate matters and non-
paying public interest cases; state officials who'd
watched her work her influence in trying to solve some
of Arkansas's most onerous problems, notably its inadequate education system. And there were, to be sure,
some who viewed her with the same skepticism they'd
shown when she had debuted in Arkansas public life
sixteen years earlier as the very independent wife of
the state's new boy wonder attorney general. As they
waited—and waited and waited—for the Clintons to
emerge and claim the victory that was already certain,
few in that crowd could have felt anything but intense
emotion. Most of it positive.

There was, for instance, Diane Blair, a University
of Arkansas political scientist who had signed on as a
Clinton friend and supporter twenty years earlier. She
gave up trying to reach the most exclusive celebration
in town being thrown by Virginia Kelley, Bill's
mother, at the Camelot Hotel. By the time Diane and
Jim Blair made it to the door, the fire marshals had
barred further entry. The Blairs worked their way
through the crowds to Clinton-Gore campaign headquarters where they settled into Diane's third-floor office and, with the janitorial crew, watched the returns
on TV.

She had spent much of the day crying, having a
"completely emotional feeling about democracy," she
said. Part of that emotion had been triggered by a
telephone call from Hillary shortly after she and Bill

had reached home from all points everywhere. "Dear friend," as Blair paraphrased Hillary's greeting, "how are you? And tell me about your wonderful children." Said Blair: "I thought, 'She is about to become First Lady and she is calling *me* to see how I have survived all of this?' It was almost as if she was saying, 'I want to remember now what the real world is like.'"

There were plenty of ordinary people who had spent their lives trying to overcome the inferiority complex that goes with a hard-pressed rural Southern state where the indifference and bias of their own political leaders too often offered little hope in their 156-year history. The most bruising insults, though, had come from supposedly enlightened men. "Bush spent the whole year making fun of us, and Perot called us chicken pluckers," Judith Woodward, a Little Rock high school teacher, told *The New York Times*. "Maybe now people will see Arkansas is like everyplace else. We're good people here. If we can produce Bill Clinton, that's our statement to the country."

At Virginia Kelley's party, about 250 relatives and Friends of Bill and Friends of Hillary and, most coveted, Friends of Both, waited their turn to see the Clintons in person. They had given up on the idea of catching Bill's speech at the Old Statehouse when it became apparent that the first party they went to would also be the only one.

"I knew a good son would go to his mother's party," said Betsy Johnson Ebeling, Hillary's childhood friend, who with her husband and about thirty of their Park Ridge friends had flown to Little Rock earlier in the day. They had known Hillary back when politics was a social science lesson, not a calling, when they were chips off their parents' conservative blocks, when she was the high school's best-known Goldwater Girl, the one who wanted to be an astronaut, then a doctor, then a lawyer living in Georgetown someday married to a U.S. senator. They had watched her become famous though it never seemed to change her. She still called them up out of the blue, wrote them notes, exchanged Christmas cards, turned up at class reunions.

Over here was Ernest "Rick" Ricketts, maybe her Park Ridge pal of longest standing, certainly her very first date. Over there was Sherry Heiden, who was always splitting planarian in biology class and the one who became a pediatric geneticist. Back there was Ebeling, who suffered through piano duets and tennis lessons with Hillary and, years later, on outings to the Great America amusement park with their kids, always was "doing the wet rides, Hillary doing the dry rides," in what Ebeling called a routine "division of labor."

And in that Camelot Hotel ballroom where still more states and numbers rolled across a giant TV screen, who of that Park Ridge group could miss the Reverend Don Jones, the long-ago "chancellor" of their University of Life youth group at the First United Methodist Church in Park Ridge? Jones had been one of the key influences in Hillary Diane Rodham's life, showing her and her friends that for many youngsters their age there was a world of despair and deprivation beyond the manicured lawns and backyard swings of Park Ridge. "He just was relentless in telling us that to be a Christian did not just mean you were concerned about your own personal salvation," Hillary told *Newsweek* in one of her many personally conducted "tours" that year.

Shortly before eleven o'clock Arkansas time on that increasingly cold November night, the networks declared Clinton the next president. The Clintons were at the Governor's Mansion, but by 11:25 the limousines carrying them, Tipper and Al Gore, and all their jubilant relatives reached the Old Statehouse. It was where Bill Clinton had declared his candidacy thirteen months earlier and where, to record this moment in American political history, a zillion watts of television illumination turned night back into day.

"Today," said William Jefferson Clinton, child of Hope and hope of 43,720,375 voting Americans, "the steelworker and the stenographer, the teacher and the nurse, had as much power in the mystery of our democracy as the president, the billionaire and the governor. You all spoke with equal voices for change. And tomorrow we will try to give you that."

And what about his outspoken, smart, determined partner who not for one moment throughout that year had thought of herself as merely "some little woman standing by my man, like Tammy Wynette"? Who had been there when the going was roughest as the Gennifer Flowers accusations threatened to destroy them both? Who calmly and convincingly had told nearly twenty-one million television viewers one January night after the 1992 Super Bowl that she loved and respected her husband, honored what he'd been through and what they'd been through together? What about her?

"She will be one of the greatest first ladies in the history of the republic," said her husband, introducing her to the world.

"Hil-la-ry!" the crowd started to chant.

Back at the Camelot, watching the big-screen TV, some friends decided that Hillary, standing beside Bill and Chelsea, looked as relaxed, happy and at peace with herself as they had seen her for the better part of a year. And, somebody also figured out why Bill looked different: for the first time in all the years they had known him, he wasn't campaigning.

When the Clintons and the Gores finally arrived at Virginia Kelley's party in the Camelot, they were supposed to remain confined to a cordoned-off aisle through the crowd—security now taking on a whole new, stifling dimension. But Hillary would have none of it and crawled under the rope to mug and hug and pose with her old Park Ridge gang in what, for the moment, was something of a gesture of defiance.

This was the Hillary who didn't take no for an answer, relished challenge, knew who she was, what she stood for, what her goals were and could strategize how to attain them—whether by ducking under a rope or making her "voice for change" heard. Among Bill Clinton's "priorities is dealing with the health care system," she had said that day in Cleveland.

"And I am particularly adamant that whatever we do, we focus on maternal and child health care," she continued, "because if we had a decent prenatal care system and early childhood health care system we would be saving money in a relatively short period of time. So if health care is one of those top priorities, the particular needs of children and women will be a big priority within that. And that's one of the things I will work on."

Not to take a stand or try to do something about that, in contrast to some of her tradition-bound predecessors at the White House, would be unthinkable.

"The kind of disconnect between rhetoric and action, between political expediency and achievement is just not going to be there," she said. "I mean, if all I thought was going to happen was moving into the White House and going to Camp David for the weekends and having a ceremonial role, I think that neither [Bill] nor I nor the Gores would be there. I mean, that is just not what's at stake in this election."

This, then, was the Hillary Clinton whom Richard Nixon had had cause to worry about, the same Hillary whose mother long ago taught her never to run from a neighborhood bully. And a good thing she did, too.

There were going to be a lot of bullies in the neighborhood around the White House.

# 2

# The Making
# of a
# Politician

*"I evolved my own political beliefs, which frankly,
in some ways . . . weren't dogmatically Republican,
dogmatically Democrat, easily defined as
liberal or conservative."*

POLITICS. THAT'S REALLY what she was about. When she was nine years old and trying to decide whether Dwight Eisenhower was a better president than Harry Truman. When she was fourteen and wondering why only boys could be astronauts. When she was seventeen and asking how she, a committed, banner-wearing Goldwater Girl, could possibly take the role of Lyndon Johnson in a high school debate.

"I can't do that," said Hillary Diane Rodham, balking at the assignment given by her government teachers at Maine Township High School South in Park Ridge, Illinois. "Oh, yes, you can," they told her. "You will now go to the library and you will now read about the other side of everything you have refused to look at for your entire life."

Hillary remembered that she and classmate Ellen Press Murdoch, an equally committed Lyndon Johnson girl told to play Barry Goldwater, "went ballistic" over their assignments. "With our teeth gritted," as Hillary later described the encounter, she and Murdoch squared off to argue the key issues of the 1964 presidential campaign.

It was the beginning of "what an education should do," she said, forcing her to read and examine opinions that weren't hers because teachers were always demanding answers to those basic and brilliant questions such as "Why do you believe this? What's the point? What's the basis?" Those same fundamental, "hard questions," she said, that demanded copious research and reflective answers, provided the approach she would take throughout her life. To reach conclusions, the course would be "Don't just tell me what I should believe, don't just tell me what the correct position is. . . . Show me what it's based on. Show me why it works and will make life better."

"I firmly believe," she told a group of Maine South students on a return visit in 1992, "that the whole purpose of politics—and it's not just elective politics on a presidential or gubernatorial level but politics with a small p—is how people get together, how they agree upon their goals, how they move together to realize those goals, how they make the absolutely inevitable tradeoffs between deeply held beliefs that are incompatible."

✳　✳　✳

When Hillary was growing up, Park Ridge was an upper-middle-class, strongly Republican suburb just northwest of Chicago where people built bomb shelters in their basements, warned their children against the menace of Communism and never let them forget their duty to God, country and family. "We would always be engaged in a struggle with Communism—that would determine our entire lives," Hillary remembered her ninth-grade social studies teacher telling the class. "That was pounded into us. That was the worldview we were given."

Current events were standard dinner table fare in most households, including the Rodhams', where Hillary's father, Hugh, a hardworking Chicago businessman, was a gruff and unyielding conservative Republican influence. Hillary's mother told Rick Ricketts, a classmate of Hillary, that she was the Democrat, though it wasn't something she spread around. "I imagine the Republican side was articulated a lot more often than the Democratic side, but I'm sure that every now and again Mrs. Rodham would set Hillary straight," said Ricketts. "My mom was a Democrat, too, but it wasn't popular to say so. You had to be careful about that. Park Ridge was as conservative as Orange County."

Whether she understood them or not, Hillary's political beliefs mirrored her father's when she was in high school. She handed out Goldwater literature, hung his campaign posters and became known around Maine South as a highly vocal Republican. It was no laughing matter then, though she could laugh about it later. "How was it," she'd say, asking the question before anyone else could, "that a nice conservative Republican girl from Park Ridge went so wrong?" Hillary admitted that "it was one of the great unanswered questions" in view of her reputation as not just a liberal Democrat but, at some points in her life, a radical one at that. "I have to tell you," she explained during her Maine South confessional, "it started right here."

The year was 1964. The growing school district of Maine Township had just opened its newest high school, Maine South, and Hillary was in the first senior class. She was taking a basic course in government from Gerald E. Baker, a young Northwestern University graduate. The presidential campaign, the first Baker had been interested in as an adult, was in full swing.

Arizona Senator Barry Goldwater's creed—"Extremism in defense of liberty is no vice . . . moderation in pursuit of justice is no virtue"—had become part of the conservatives' dogma. He railed against expanding federal power and ranted on behalf of a dynamic strategy against Communism. President Lyndon Johnson stumped the country to sell what would become his Great Society's goals of equal opportunities for all and the elimination of unemployment and poverty.

All of this was played against the Democrats' masterfully crafted paid television message picturing the horrors of nuclear war, a not-so-subtle reminder of where "extremism in the defense of liberty" could lead. The prospect was disquieting to America's voters. To their children, even conservative ones in Park Ridge, the mushroom clouds were terrifyingly real.

Throughout that September and October, Gerald Baker discussed the campaign with his students. "I liked to talk about issues and get the kids thinking," he said. "Hillary was very up to speed on issues and very articulate about her views on things. I used to tease her a little and she would get pretty frustrated with me because I was of the Kennedy philosophy. The dichotomy between us was obvious. Philosophically or politically, she and I didn't see eye to eye on much."

Then, as the race headed into the home stretch, Baker saw a chance to engage Maine South's student body in the political process by organizing a schoolwide voter registration drive, a debate about each candidate's position and a mock election. For students like Hillary, it seemed a natural way for them to put what they were learning in class into practice. "I thought this mock election would be right up Hillary's alley," said Baker.

The debate took place at the end of October. The mock election followed two days later. The outcome was not surprising to anyone familiar with the politics of Park Ridge. Students voted for Goldwater by a 55 percent to 45 percent margin. When their parents went to the polls a few days later, they gave him a 58 percent margin over Johnson's 42 percent. Nationally, Johnson swept to victory by winning 61 percent of the vote, and Park Ridge had the dubious distinction of being among the 38 percent that voted for Goldwater. They had one consolation, however. Their children had kept the faith.

Baker judged the mock election a success but the debate a disappointment. As Goldwater, Murdoch had had a decided advantage in a community traditionally

Republican. As Johnson, Hillary, even then a commanding speaker, had fought a losing battle. Because of lack of interest by some students and premature decisions by others, Baker later announced, the debate had not "fulfilled" its purpose. (Despite Murdoch's teenage reputation as a "bleeding-heart liberal," she would actually turn Republican in later years. When Bill Clinton became president in 1993, Murdoch began the final year of a Bush administration appointment as chairman of the Pentagon's Defense Advisory Committee on Women in the Service.)

Hillary's take on politics, the kind "with a small p," started long before she ever became interested in elective politics—with the "capital P." Her early politics was an amalgam of childhood influences—her family, school and church. By the time she reached college, she told those Maine South students, she was "still a Republican but with a different kind of attitude and a different sort of inquiry about what it was I believed. I evolved my own political beliefs, which frankly, in some ways . . . weren't dogmatically Republican, dogmatically Democrat, easily defined as liberal or conservative."

Her upbringing in the Methodist church was a significant factor in how she viewed politics. "As I grew and studied on my own, I found the approach of Methodism to appeal to me and to be very compatible to my life," Hillary told Jean Lyles for the United Methodist News Service in 1992. "On my first personal faith journey and my social commitments, the emphasis on personal salvation and active applied Christianity . . . the practical method of trying to live as a Christian in a difficult, challenging world, was very appealing to me."

She was two months old when her father and mother took her to Scranton, Pennsylvania, so she could be christened in the Court Street Methodist Church where Hugh Rodham had worshipped as a child. The Methodism of Hillary's father was of the Wesleyan tradition. Hillary was fascinated by his Welsh forebears and their ties to one of Methodism's sacred shrines, Bristol, England, where its founder, John Wesley, spent much of his itinerant ministry. Around Scranton in the early part of the twentieth century it wasn't unusual for Methodists to seek salvation in the evangelical tradition at revival meetings. Hillary's mother, with English and Canadian roots, was more mainstream Methodist.

Hillary was Dorothy and Hugh E. Rodham's first child and only daughter and she was born on October 26, 1947, at Chicago's Edgewater Hospital on the city's North Side. No lightweight even then, she pushed the scales at eight pounds eight ounces. Dorothy wanted her name to be something different so she chose Hillary because besides having family significance it was often given to boys. Dorothy liked that.

(In one of those geographical coincidences, the Rodhams lived for a time at 5722 North Winthrop in the Edgewater area of Chicago, not all that far from the home Bill Clinton's father, William Blythe, had bought for his wife, Virginia, and the child they were expecting. His address was listed as 3517 West Madison, a few miles southwest of Edgewater, on the May 17, 1946, report of his death filed by the Missouri

State Highway Patrol. Three months before Bill was born—and seventeen months before Hillary was born—Blythe was killed three miles west of Sikeston, Missouri, when his fast-moving car apparently blew a tire and skidded off the road. He was on his way to pick up Virginia in Hope, Arkansas, and take her back to Chicago in time for the birth of their child.)

The Rodhams' second child, Hugh, born in 1950, was a babe in arms when they left their one-bedroom apartment for a twenty-five-year-old three-bedroom, two-story brick Georgian house they bought in the suburbs. Located at 236 Wisner Avenue in Park Ridge, it was part of the country club section, the same area where the founding Robb family had settled in 1832.

The Rodhams chose Park Ridge "mostly because they wanted a good school district," according to Hillary. "I mean that's what the motivation was for the ex-GIs after World War II, to try to find a good place to raise your kids and send them to school. And I've often kidded my father, who has never been a fan of taxes or government, about moving to a place that had such high property taxes to pay for school."

Hillary's mother and father were typical of the growing middle class living the good life. Dorothy Rodham was a stay-at-home mother, Hugh the breadwinner father whose textile business in Chicago did custom-made draperies for corporations, hotels and airlines. They didn't socialize much with the rest of the neighborhood but Hillary and her brothers, Hughie and Tony, seven years her junior, made up for it. "There must have been forty or fifty children within a four-block radius of our house and within four years of

Hillary's age," Dorothy Rodham told *The Washington Post*'s Martha Sherrill. "They were all together, all the time, a big extended family. There were more boys than girls, lots of playing and competition. [Hillary] held her own at cops-and-robbers, hide-and-seek, chase-and-run—all the games that children don't play anymore."

The Rodham children were expected to do non-paying household chores. At their father's shop, the boys sometimes helped and, according to Tony, "we'd get, like, an extra potato at dinner." The way they earned money, he told *People*, was in dandelion-pulling contests. "Of course, I won all the time."

Dorothy never graduated from college and was eager that her children would. When her brood was a little older, she began to make up for her own academic shortcomings by taking courses at area junior colleges. Hillary's friends were impressed and called her the all-time record-holding back-to-schooler. "That was very unusual at the time," said Betsy Johnson Ebeling, Hillary's friend from the sixth grade. "She would find things that would interest her, like Spanish. She never had enough credits to make a major because she was always finding something else she wanted to learn about."

Hugh Rodham knew only too well the value of a college education. Namesake and the second of three sons of a Scranton, Pennsylvania, lace factory supervisor whose family had emigrated from England in the late nineteenth century, Hugh once worked as a coal miner during the Depression. But he also earned a BS degree in education on a football scholarship to Pennsylvania

State University, graduating in 1935. Instead of teaching, he opted for a job with the Scranton Lace Works Company. By 1937, he was a salesman in Chicago. Years later, he showed Hillary and her brothers what life might have been like had he not gone to college. He took them to see the coal mine where he once worked.

Dorothy was born in Chicago, daughter of a fireman, but had grown up in California. Her roots were English but also Canadian. She graduated from Alhambra High School in 1937 and later that year was back in Chicago where she met twenty-five-year-old Hugh when she applied for a job as a secretary at the Columbia Lace Company. They did not marry for another five years. By then, World War II had begun. Hugh's college degree in physical education qualified him to train sailors in a U.S. Navy physical education program named after former heavyweight boxing champion Gene Tunney.

In 1950, when Dorothy and Hugh Rodham arrived in Park Ridge, it was little exaggeration to say that they'd finally found their utopia. It came with all the amenities former GIs had hoped for—good schools, good churches, good neighborhoods. The Rodhams didn't belong to the country club nearby but everything else about their lifestyle could have been lifted straight out of an *Ozzie and Harriet* TV sitcom. Comfortably middle-class, it was also comfortably white. Not until Hillary's senior year at Maine South High School would there be a black student, and he a foster child. The suburb was so different from Arkansas, the state Hillary later claimed as her own, that she would describe her move there as "a re-entrance to the human condition."

By all her own accounts, Hillary and her brothers had an idyllic childhood. They walked to Eugene Field Elementary School, spent winters ice skating and building snowmen, and the rest of the year riding their bicycles and playing on safe neighborhood streets until dusk.

Hillary and her brothers also played word games at their mother's urging, and card games that their father taught them. By an early age, Hillary had learned pinochle, a card game of some wile and cunning and as challenging to her grandfather Hugh and his adult sons as bridge was to many suburban housewives. Besides the thrill of competition, Hillary said later, pinochle was a kind of discipline that appealed to her highly organized nature, an exercise in thinking things through. The Rodham men played it so much that when she married Bill Clinton he had to learn it, too—or presumably run the risk of a lifetime in the woodshed.

Baking chocolate chip cookies, which many years later would become a bizarre litmus test of her political sensitivity, became a Christmas ritual. As she told Marian Burros for *Family Circle* in 1992, her father was such a Christmas traditionalist that he didn't believe in putting up the tree until Christmas Eve. Because his arrival with the tree invariably set off childhood pandemonium, Dorothy Rodham made chocolate chip cookies as a distraction in the kitchen. As Hillary and her brothers grew older, they all made them.

"Of course, my brothers' idea of a chocolate chip

cookie was a cookie as big as a plate and they were vying who could make the world's biggest chocolate chip," Hillary said. "Pretty soon there would be one chocolate chip cookie on a cookie sheet. We'd have so much fun. The cookie smells would fill the house and there would be tons of chocolate chip cookies, which we would eat all Christmas morning while we were playing with our toys. We'd all get sick by afternoon."

Hillary's parents, driven in their desire that their children have the best education possible, urged her to excel in sports as well as the Three Rs. If at first she did not succeed at slamming baseballs, her parents insisted she try again.

She was the heroine in a couple of favorite family melodramas. One might have been called "Hillary at the Bat," and opened with Hillary at home plate unable to hit a curveball. It was no small shortcoming in a neighborhood of boys and a family of athletes where playing ball was about winning, not just about casual pickup games after school because there wasn't anything better to do.

So after church on Sundays, the Rodhams took Hillary and headed for the park, where, in grueling batting practice, they subjected her to curveball after curveball until finally she could slam the old horsehide as well as any of the boys. She not only became a good hitter and a crack shortstop but she wound up knowing more about baseball than most of the boys she played with. "She'd ask these fairly obscure questions, like what was the 1927 Yankee batting order," said Ricketts, who lived down the street. "If I didn't know the answers, she'd get mad at me."

In the other melodrama starring Hillary, there was no room in the Rodham household for cowards. Dorothy Rodham told an interviewer how she sent her sobbing four-year-old daughter back on the street to slug it out with a female bully in the neighborhood. "The next time she hits you, I want you to hit her back," her mother told her. Hillary did, to the astonishment of young male onlookers. "I can play with the boys now!" Hillary triumphantly informed her mother. Said brother Tony: "My sister is tough as nails. She's a lot of those things that people have said she was." Added brother Hugh, to *The Washington Post*: "But that's just one facet. That's her business face. You know, like your game face when you play football?"

Hillary always considered herself "very fortunate, because as a girl growing up, I never felt anything but support from my family. Whatever I thought I could do and be, they supported. There was no distinction between me and my brothers or any barriers thrown up to me that I couldn't think about something because I was a girl. If you work hard enough and you really apply yourself then you should be able to do whatever you choose to do."

Dorothy Rodham told Lloyd Grove of *The Washington Post*: "I never saw any difference in gender, as far as capabilities or aspirations were concerned. Just because [Hillary] was a girl didn't mean she should be limited. I don't know whether you could say that was unusual at the time. I guess it was more of an accepted role to stay within your scope." And to *The New York Times*, she further explained that she was "determined that no daughter of mine was going to have to go through the agony of being afraid to say what she had on her mind."

Hillary confirmed that "when I got into high school, I saw a lot of my friends who had been really lively and smart and doing well in school beginning to worry that boys would think they were too smart, or beginning to cut back on how well they did or the courses they took, because that's not where their boyfriends were. And I can recall thinking, 'Gosh— why are they doing that?' It didn't make sense to me."

Ricketts, Hillary's classmate from fourth grade on through high school, remembered that she had strong opinions about everything, even as a nine-year-old. "She was a great debater. Sometimes she would take an opposing position just because it was fun to argue." Walking home from school, they talked about politics and whatever the current events were at the time. They both liked history. Once, he remembered, they discussed the Civil War at great length, wondering what would have happened if the South had won.

Hillary knew what she was about long before most girls her age. "At a time when all of us were checking a lot of personalities out, she was always very confident about who she was and where she was going," said Ebeling. "She was like her father that way, confident in what he believed. She got a lot of her single-mindedness from him."

Said Murdoch: "She was never subject to peer pressure. Things didn't bother her very much. She wasn't the type who would lie awake nights worrying if anybody liked her or whether she was going to get into Wellesley."

In the Maine South 1965 yearbook, Hillary's accomplishments were awesome: Class Council, junior vice president, class newspaper, Girls Athletic Association, gym leader, National Honor Society, pep club, science award, Speech Activities and Debate, spring musical, Student Council, Cultural Values Committee, Organizations Committee, variety show. She was the overachievers' overachiever, an A student in the top 5 percent of her class. Only her father professed to be unimpressed. "You must go to a pretty easy school," he would growl when she brought home her report cards.

She went through the same fads and phases other kids did—Frankie Avalon, Fabian, Ricky Nelson, the Beatles—but never Elvis Presley. She and Ebeling read Daphne du Maurier, the Hardy Boys and "gobbled up every Nancy Drew there was but our teacher didn't approve. That was too light reading," said Ebeling. Their sixth-grade teacher, Elisabeth King, was so taken with Hillary that when Hillary went into Ralph Waldo Emerson Junior High, she also transferred in order to teach her another two years. "Hillary was Mrs. King's favorite human being on earth," Ricketts told Martha Sherrill of *The Washington Post*.

King was not the only teacher to be captivated by Hillary. Marlan Davis, in his thirty-five years of teaching secondary-school English, remembered her as exceptional, with an "incisive and intuitive mind, a voracious appetite for challenge, boundless energy and a puckish sense of humor." An advance-placement English course that Davis taught seniors preparing to go on to college required the standard fare of Shakespeare, Conrad and Dante. Davis gave the exam in mid-May 1965 and remembered that Hillary arrived early to string up a homemade banner on which she had lettered the warning above Dante's Gates of Hell in *The Inferno*: "All hope abandon, ye who enter here."

She was a first-rate ham, according to Murdoch. As co-director of Maine South's first annual variety show, a retrospective of American history, Murdoch wrote Hillary and several of their best friends into one skit about temperance. Nobody played parts, which was just as well, since Hillary, at least, would have been too short to try out for the six-foot-tall Carry Nation, the temperance leader. But Hillary was every bit as passionate as Carry had been in her heyday, laying waste to iniquitous nineteenth-century saloons. And Hillary was the picture of moral rectitude in her prim dress and funny hat as she and the others sang with outraged voices about the sinful wages of demon rum. "Alcohol!" spat out Hillary at one point. "The very word sticks in my throat and renders me weak with disgust."

Alcohol, in fact, was not a problem for Hillary's crowd and drugs had not yet come along. In health class, they all saw a film about the dangers of marijuana. "But it didn't seem to have very much to do with us," said Murdoch. If the girls were addicted to anything, it was slumber parties where the talk focused on boys; who was in, who wasn't; and the universe, in general. Hillary loved to talk.

"She had a large and inquiring mind about everything," said Sherry Heiden, who became the doctor that Hillary once had thought she wanted to be— to the point where Hillary even took an advanced-placement course in biology in order to fulfill the necessary college entrance requirements. "Her scope was always global. She was like her mom, who always wanted to know everything about everything." Said Hillary's brother Tony: "When she wasn't studying, she was a lot of fun. But she was always studying."

Gregarious by nature, she had many friends, girls and boys, and kept in touch with them over the years. "She's very hardworking at friendship," said Ebeling. "All of a sudden you realize six months have gone by and you haven't talked and then the phone will ring and it's Hillary."

She was the one who tried to keep everybody on track in group efforts, and when she wasn't successful would be visibly frustrated. "Don't you want to be good?" she might plead in a rehearsal when everybody else was horsing around.

Somehow she missed a gawky adolescence. Pictures of her from that period show her as a pretty girl, with even features, an easy smile and blue eyes that danced. But she was terribly nearsighted. "I think some people thought she was conceited because she wouldn't say hello to them, but she couldn't see," said Ebeling. "So when she ran for student council, I was her campaign manager because I could see." Her hair was blond and straight, pulled back at times and at others framing her face. She was a saddle-shoes or white-bucks-and-sailor-dress-type in grammar school.

In high school, she wore loafers with her skirts and sweaters.

Her dating habits reflected a certain sophistication and, in the eyes of some girlfriends, she came across as "glamorous" and "coolly in control." "None of my kids dated much, until they were older," said Dorothy Rodham. "And Hillary always valued herself very highly. I liked that about her."

The very first date she had was in 1961 with Ricketts, whom she asked to take her to a Girl's Choice dance. Later, said one friend, Hillary preferred the company of older boys who had already graduated. One was a local youth who went to Princeton and later became a doctor. "Part of it," explained the friend, "was when you're a very intelligent girl at the age of seventeen, most seventeen-year-old boys don't have a lot to offer right then. Most of the boys our own age were okay, but not very exciting."

Hillary became proficient at almost anything she tried—with the exception of piano, and also, if her husband could be believed, driving a car. In a recital duet with Ebeling, Hillary had not bothered to learn the bass but merely repeated the same notes, speeding up or slowing down the tempo according to Ebeling's lead.

And Hillary was a junior at the other high school, Maine East, when Kenneth Reese, student counselor, taught the classroom phase of her course in driver education. "She got some of the basics from me," Reese said. "Bill Clinton said he thought the Maine system was a pretty good high school. But when he learned that we taught her to drive, he said maybe he had some second thoughts about that."

Sports excited her. Part of it may have been the challenge of competing and the determination to win in a family of two macho brothers egged on by their former football star father. At the insistence of Ellen Murdoch, Hillary joined the Mariner Scouts. They learned to sail on a little lake at the edge of Park Ridge and to canoe on the Des Plaines River, deliberately "drown-proofing" themselves to prove they could bring their capsized canoes upright again.

She was a certified swimming instructor who taught young children in a recreation department summer program. And she considered herself good enough at tennis to draw up a contract pledging to teach Ebeling. It may have been the first contract she ever drafted. It was not, however, the only clue that she might be interested in the law.

In a spoof interview she wrote about herself for Maine South's student newspaper in December 1964, Hillary "reviewed" her high school career from the vantage point of "a prosecuting attorney" working on a case that had been going on "literally for years." One last question at the end proved particularly illuminating: What was her ambition in high school? "To marry a senator and settle down in Georgetown," she said.

She was fascinated by words. "She was an exceptional student," said Pauline Yates, who, in Hillary's freshman year, taught grammar and composition with an emphasis on clarity of expression and the importance of being terse. It was Hillary's ability to analyze and reach her own conclusions that stuck with Otto Kohler, head of the English department.

The "absolute turning point" in her life, Hillary said, came in November 1963 when she was sixteen and John F. Kennedy was assassinated in Dallas. "Whether you were for him politically or against him," she told her Maine South audience in 1992, Kennedy's death seemed to focus the troubles of the time and those to come: the assassinations of Martin Luther King and Robert F. Kennedy, the 1968 riots, the Vietnam War, the civil rights revolution, the women's movement, the Watergate break-in and impeachment proceedings, the drop in the standard of living.

Kennedy had never been popular in Park Ridge, though for younger people in some Republican households there had been a certain glamorous panache associated with his family and his New Frontier programs. The Peace Corps would eventually lure Hillary's brother Hugh into its ranks. And earlier, as the space program offered seemingly limitless horizons, Hillary had written to NASA asking what she should do to be an astronaut. NASA's reply, itself an object lesson for a future feminist, was that " 'We are not accepting girls as astronauts.' Which was very infuriating," Hillary told *The Washington Post*.

The day word raced through Maine East's corridors that Kennedy had been shot in Dallas, "we were all horrified," said Murdoch, recalling a hastily called school assembly to confirm that Kennedy had died. "To have everything fall apart in the course of one day was disturbing and distressing. I don't think it ever occurred to any of us that presidents got shot."

The Rodham family's church, the First United Methodist, reacted swiftly. Rosalie Benzinger, then director of Christian education, and others on the staff sent messages to the nearly three thousand member congregation. "It was an attempt to help people see that we should not lay blame on any particular group," she said. "What we were afraid of at that point was that everybody would say the Communists had done it. We were trying to help them see that evil does lurk in the hearts of man and these things happen, that it was important to learn from it and move on. We knew that the children would certainly be traumatized by it and we were simply trying to help form some attitudes that would be helpful rather than harmful."

Supported by what Benzinger described as "an upwardly mobile congregation who took the same kind of attitude about their church that they took about their work," the Park Ridge Methodist church boasted the largest Sunday school in the Chicago area, with a reputation among Christian academics for providing a "status" education program. Hillary was eleven years old when, along with 110 other youths, she was confirmed on March 22, 1959, by the Reverend Guy Morrison, youth minister.

Though the bitter realities of America's social ills would begin to haunt Hillary and her contemporaries in the decade to come, there were no such doubts then. "When you grow up in a protected suburb," said classmate Heiden, "you can't imagine what's out there unless someone brings you to it."

The "someone" who brought Hillary to what was "out there" was the new youth minister who arrived in Park Ridge in September 1961. He was the Reverend Don Jones, a recent graduate of Drew University Seminary, a four-year navy veteran and, by his own "admission," an existentialist. At the time, existentialism was commonly viewed as an obscure, even dangerous European influence or philosophy. Jones explained it as "a mode of thinking that emphasizes decision-making, commitment and responsibility for one's own existence with a focus on such themes as anxiety, tragedy, finitude, human freedom, the uniqueness of the self, and the conflict between the counterfeit and authentic self."

Other influences on Jones were such theologians as Dietrich Bonhoeffer, who unrelentingly pointed out that the role of the Christian was a moral one of total engagement in the world promoting human development, and Reinhold Niebuhr, whose ideas combined a healthy pessimism about human nature with a passion for justice and social reform.

Hillary had never met anyone like Jones.

He devised a series of Sunday and Thursday evening programs, weekend retreats and educational and social action projects. He called it the University of Life, and he encouraged the kids to simply drop in to see him after school. And, indeed, at that time, the Park Ridge church had placed little emphasis on social action, prophetic criticism of society or radical interpretations of the Christian faith. Jones was eager to work with these youths, in hopes they would face "the human situation with utter realism, have the experience of social service and help people directly, and through it all become aware of life outside Park Ridge."

Ricketts remembered that Jones once arranged for his group to hear an atheist debate a Christian over the existence of God. Another time, there was a discussion of teenage pregnancy "which got the whole congregation upset." To further heighten awareness, Jones used art as a teaching tool, introducing his students to the works of French film director François Truffaut, poet e. e. cummings, novelist J. D. Salinger and artist Pablo Picasso. For its time, this was radical education: to see a foreign film about an abused Paris urchin who ended up in jail; to read *Catcher in the Rye* banned by libraries because of its occasional use of profanity; to read a poet who didn't capitalize words; and to study a painting about alienation, tragedy and killing—in the company of a group of inner-city Chicago youths whose own lives were filled with alienation, tragedy and even killing.

Jones arranged a trip to the Chicago ghetto so his suburban charges could meet with a group of black youths who hung around a recreation center. "It wasn't a social worker kind of thing where we talked about our differences—what it's like to be black and what it's like to be white," said Jones. "It was indirect and existential." For Hillary, the experience was profound. "It just kind of opened up my mind," she said later.

In one inner-city session, Jones leaned his print of Picasso's *Guernica* against the back of a chair and suggested that the two groups look at it in silence for a few minutes. When he opened the discussion, he

asked what images disturbed them. Someone men-
tioned the light bulb, another the broken arm, someone else the baby and the mother crying. When he
asked what music they would set to it, what title
they would attach, one youth said the Rolling Stones's
"Satisfaction," someone else the blues, yet another a
classical work.

"Then I got down to more subjective things,"
Jones said. "I'd say, 'Does anything about this painting
remind you of something that you've experienced or
observed?' And then the inner-city kids had more to
say than the suburban kids. I remember one young girl
asking why her uncle had to die, that 'just last week
my uncle drove up and parked on the street and some
guy came up to him and said you can't park there,
that's my parking place. And my uncle resisted him
and the guy pulled out a gun and shot him.' "

For these privileged Park Ridge kids living in
what Rosalie Benzinger called "almost a cellophaned
envelope, protected from so many of the things other
kids were experiencing," such encounters with black
youngsters weren't just rare. They were nonexistent. If
there was no overt racism in the community, Benzinger
remembered that there was "real concern on the part
of some people when they would hear that a black
family was going to move into town. People got very
unnerved because they were afraid it was going to affect
property values, which was one of the reasons we at
the church were trying to do what we did about those
attitudes."

One of Hillary's earliest experiences with disadvantaged minority youngsters occurred in 1960 when

she was thirteen and joined a baby-sitting brigade of other young girls organized by the church to look after children of migrant farm workers. To harvest the crops on truck farms a short distance south and west of Park Ridge, blacks and Hispanics moved up from Southern states during summer months. The earning period was brief and whole families took to the fields, often leaving younger children alone or in the care of one another.

It was an alien world to Hillary and an early glimpse of poverty. To learn of society's inequities and see its young and helpless victims at close range, in time would take on both spiritual and intellectual dimensions.

She was a "budding intellectual," Jones said, "but she was much more than that. She was also on a kind of spiritual quest, open to the fullness of life, including the various cultural and theological materials used in this youth ministry." Sometimes she stopped in to see him just to talk about those things.

One day he reached back and pulled off the shelf *Catcher in the Rye*, urging her to read it because he thought she would like it. She read it but Jones learned later that she didn't like it. In one of her letters from college, she told of rereading it during the summer and being struck by how much Holden Caulfield reminded her of her brother Hughie. "Both of them love life and people almost to the point of reverence," she wrote, adding that it had probably been too advanced for her at the age of fifteen but that on second reading she appreciated it.

Whatever impact the book had on Hillary, and Jones never knew that for certain, he later saw as pertinent the correlation between the novel's emphsais on young children and Hillary's subsequent commitment to children's issues. "The very title of the book" Jones regarded as symbolic, as it had "to do with Holden's fantasy about standing on the edge of 'some crazy cliff' in a field of rye catching the children before they would fall off."

Still full of his own seminary studies, Jones had his youth group reading weighty theologians, hoping he could help them see that Christianity "was not just about personal salvation and pious escapism, but also about an authentic and deep quest for God and life's meaning in the midst of worldly existence." He would take passages from a sermon by Paul Tillich, who believed one encounters God in crisis, chart them on a blackboard and go over them line by line. And how did Hillary respond to such a radical approach to faith? Jones said he never knew other than that "she seemed to thrive on it."

Hillary was fifteen when Jones shepherded his youth group into Chicago on April 15, 1962, to hear the Reverend Martin Luther King, Jr. Freedom rides had been going on in the South for several years but Congress would not pass the Civil Rights Act for another two years.

Six weeks earlier, an Albany, Georgia, city court had found King guilty of parading without a permit, disturbing the peace, and obstructing the sidewalk in a mass demonstration to desegregate public facilities and register black voters. His sentence had been held in abeyance, and in the weeks that followed he made a cross-country speaking and concert tour to raise money for bail and legal fees on behalf of several hundred blacks who had been arrested throughout that winter in the Albany Movement.

That April night in Chicago, some 2,500 people packed Orchestra Hall where the nondenominational Sunday Evening Club series had been drawing crowds since it was founded in 1907. King's message, titled "Remaining Awake through a Revolution," a theme he would come back to again and again before he died six years later, was an urgent one urging Americans "to eradicate the last vestiges of racial injustice from our nation . . . [and] that racial injustice is still the black man's burden and the white man's shame."

The speech galvanized his listeners, among them young Hillary Rodham. Jones had made arrangements for his group to meet King, and after the speech was over Hillary and the others inched their way through the crowd to where he was waiting to shake their hands. The meeting was only too brief but Hillary never forgot it and would tell Jones later that it was a seminal event in her life.

Jones left Park Ridge in September 1963 to begin graduate studies at Drew University but Hillary was determined to stay in touch. Writing a four-page letter to him in May 1964, she told of losing an election for the presidency of the Student Council but then being elected chair of the Organizations Committee, which meant she got to "organize the council and help write the constitution." She noted that the latter campaign had ended up being "pretty dirty," with her opponent's campaign manager "slinging mud" at her. She also talked about being in charge of the junior-senior prom,

going on television with five other classmates to talk
about "teenage values," and giving a speech at a junior
high school the following week.

She brought Jones up to date on the Methodist
youth group, telling him that one of her friends was
elected president of the University of Life and that
another, Rick Ricketts, was the new retreat chairman.
"We are going to have some sharp retreats!" she predicted. She wasn't getting along too well with the new
youth minister, however. "I think he believes I'm a
little radical," she said.

At the end, she implored Jones to "please write.
I love to get mail from intelligent people."

That fall, Hillary was an outspoken Goldwater
Republican, the seeming antithesis of everything that
the University of Life had tried to teach. But she was
not to escape the cumulative effect of Martin Luther
King, the ghetto youths and migrant children.

She would be going to college in September 1965
and had narrowed her choice to several women's colleges, the Seven Sisters, scattered around New England. She was a prize student, sought after by
Chicago-area Smith and Wellesley alumnae who invited her to get-acquainted teas and receptions. "It
was all very rich and fancy," she said later, "and very
intimidating to my way of thinking."

Two young Smith and Wellesley graduates were
teaching at Maine South that year. One was Janet
Altman Spragens, a student teacher from Northwestern
who had grown up in Washington, D.C., and had
graduated from Wellesley in 1964. Spragens remem-

bered that Hillary approached her one day to ask about Wellesley.

"She was very smart, very thoughtful, very receptive to new ideas," said Spragens. "This was in the heart of a strong conservative Republican political philosophy. My impression was that very few kids went east to the Ivy League, so that was really a departure for her, a break. I thought it would be a broadening of her background, and though I didn't know her parents I thought it was a mark of their thinking that they would let her go east to this women's college. The Ivy League schools were gender-segregated and for women to receive an education of similar quality they had to go to the Seven Sisters."

Spragens, who later became a professor of law at American University, said she may have told Hillary that Wellesley was near Boston, with all the advantages of the city, and that Smith was in the much more rural location of Northampton, Massachusetts. "I don't recall trying to twist her arm to go to Wellesley."

Nor did Spragens tell Hillary she couldn't go to Yale or Brown or any of those all-male schools. "I just said Wellesley offered an extraordinarily high-quality education, that it had enormous resources, stressed the importance of women's education and women's role in society, that very talented women went there, and that I was sure she would make important lifetime friends."

Gerald Baker, Hillary's government teacher, who was later to become chief lobbyist for the Airline Pilots Association in Washington, D.C., had followed her search for a college with more than casual interest. "I used to chide Hillary and say, 'You're going to go to Wellesley and you're going to become a liberal and a Democrat.' And she used to get irritated at me and say things like 'I'm smart' and 'I know where I stand on the issues and that's not going to change.'

"But, of course," Baker added, "she did change."

# 3

# *An Activist in the Making*

*"I wonder if it's possible to be a mental conservative
and a heart liberal?"*

PHOTOGRAPHS OF HILLARY RODHAM from her years at Wellesley College reveal the face of a poised, reflective and unself-consciously pretty young woman, possessing what high school classmate Ellen Press Murdoch called "an amazing presence." Murdoch remembered talking to her about her Wellesley application. "One of the questions on it was 'How do you deal with defeat?'—which would have completely undone me. But Hillary's answer, she said, was 'Philosophically.'"

Of course, "defeat" was hardly a word in Hillary Rodham's vocabulary, even at that point in her life. Her graduation from high school was almost embarrassing to her parents as they watched her troop back

and forth to the stage accepting awards for everything
from National Merit Scholar finalist to National Honor
Society. She only had been away from home with girlfriends on a few trips, and until the Rodhams drove
her to Wellesley, never for any extended period. It was
"really, really hard to leave her," Dorothy Rodham
told *The Washington Post*'s Martha Sherrill. "After we
dropped her off, I just crawled in the back seat and
cried for eight hundred miles."

Now, on September 12, 1965, Hillary was entering one of the country's most prestigious women's colleges, one of the Seven Sisters, at a time when "sister"
was about to take on a more intricate political meaning.

"We arrived not yet knowing what was not possible," she recalled later. "Consequently, we expected a
lot." Wellesley, on the other hand, welcomed them
as it always had their predecessors, confident of its
reputation for taking the daughters of the country's
elite and upper middle class and producing impressive
women leaders by exposing them to both some of the
best minds in the country and a rigid sense of social
tradition.

For almost a century, Wellesley had played a
historical role in the country's patriarchal society, giving women who were bright and wanted to make something of their lives a vision and a way to do that but
within the traditional understanding of women in the
world. "Women can do the work. I give them the
chance," said Henry Fowle Durant, who founded
Wellesley in 1875.

The college motto, *"Non Ministrari sed Mi-
nistrare,"* reflected the New Testament injunction to

give of oneself and one's service, not to be ministered unto but to minister (inevitably translated by polite, cultured if waggish young women as "not to be ministers but to be ministers' wives"). From well-to-do Protestant families, for the most part, generations had come to this picture-perfect campus outside Boston and taken with them a strong commitment to serve.

Unlike the fresh suburban feel of Maine South High School where customs were only then being established, Hillary found herself in a Wellesley rooted in the white-gloved afternoon-tea-with-one-lump-or-two traditions of gracious and proper living. Cloistered in venerable academia, freshmen wore beanies, everybody wore skirts to dinner and seniors rolled hoops to determine—legend had it—who among them would be the first bride after graduation.

Now, though, there was a sense of transition. By the time of her graduation four years later, Hillary could sum up the experience with clarity: "Both the college and the country were going through a period of rapid, sometimes tumultuous changes. . . . My classmates and I felt challenged and, in turn, challenged the college from the moment we arrived. Nothing was taken for granted."

As with most colleges, Wellesley's administrators felt an absolute responsibility to determine rules about dress and parietal privileges, required courses and admissions practices. Hillary and her classmates were among the first to question this with any effectiveness. "You have to imagine what Wellesley College was like traditionally," said Stephen London, who had Hillary as a student in the first class he ever taught at Wellesley on urban sociology. "To have a sense that students had any say at all in decisions regarding their own destiny, both in a larger society and in the academic world itself, was something of a new thought—to put it mildly."

Some of the issues were apparent from the moment the Class of 1969 unpacked its bags. Geography had always been a consideration in recruiting new students, with the idea of forming a diverse student body, race a lesser one. Diversity had its limits, however: arriving on campus, freshmen drew room assignments dictated by color and religion.

"I was the first black freshman to have a white roommate, but I didn't realize there was anything unusual about this until talking to my roommate," recalled Francille Rusan Wilson, one of a half dozen black students entering with the Class of 1969. "The college had even called her to ask if this was okay. They [traditionally] roomed Jewish students with Jewish students, Episcopalians with Episcopalians. We were really appalled. They hadn't done it because they ran out of rooms. They told her it was an experiment." The roommate was Eleanor Dean Acheson, granddaughter of Dean Acheson, President Truman's secretary of state, and later a close friend of Hillary Rodham's.

Out of this incident came Ethos, a tiny band of ten women who made up the school's entire black enrollment and who set out to draw attention to a variety of grievances. It was not easy in an environment where information was rigorously controlled. "You couldn't speak to reporters about something you were doing without the college's permission. They were very nervous about any negative publicity, and of course it made them very vulnerable to those of us who were activists," said Wilson.

Demonstrations, however, were not the Wellesley way. Disgruntled women there seemed more focused on internal reform of the school than the broader social issue questions of the time such as the Vietnam War. And leading many of these discussions was Hillary Rodham. Some classmates remember Hillary speaking out against the irrelevance of some courses required in certain study areas to graduate. "There aren't many people here," Hillary complained to her audience, standing around her in a campus parking lot, "because they're all in the library working on their distribution requirements."

Hillary's initial activism was aimed at partisan politics. She joined the campus Republican club and was immediately elected president. "It wasn't very large. I think that's why," recalled a fellow member. Size had nothing to do with fervor. Hillary and her GOP cohorts did the grunt work for Republican candidates—"The girl who doesn't want to go out and shake hands can type letters or do general office work," she urged—and in the 1965–66 campaign of then-Massachusetts Attorney General Edward Brooke for United States Senate Hillary may have been among those responsible for sending him to Washington. In one of those curious ironies, they would share the commencement day platform four years later when, as Wellesley's first student ever to deliver a commencement speech, she would gain national attention for passionately, if delicately, impaling him for his pro forma address to her and her classmates, his "empty rhetoric," as she called it.

Friends remembered her as an eloquent exponent of the question "Why Be a Republican?" Classmate Constance Hoenk Shapiro, a Democrat who heard her speak their freshman year, recalled thinking, "I disagree with many of the things she said but she is very articulate." Acheson, who took a freshman political science class with Hillary in which classmates described their political backgrounds, was "shocked to find out that not just Hillary but other very smart people were Republican." Acheson told *The Boston Globe* it had "depressed" her but that "it did explain why they won presidential elections from time to time."

It was clear to some of Hillary's classmates, one of them Kristine Olson Rogers, that even in her freshman year "political science was a passion." Rogers's first memory of Hillary came as they sat in her room talking about politics. "She was an avid student of government," said Rogers. "She was so earnest, so interested, so much attuned to what was going on in the world."

But it was more than just the mechanics of politics or government that interested Hillary. Even in her early years at Wellesley, government seemed to be a means for accomplishing bigger ends. She continued to correspond with the Reverend Don Jones, her Park Ridge youth minister.

In April 1966, Hillary wrote Jones to say how exciting college was because it enabled her to try out different identities. Her January identity, she said, had been her determination to spend every organized minute studying. Which she did. Then, "after six weeks of little human communication or companion-ship, my diet [of reading and writing] gave me indiges-tion. The last two weeks of February here were an orgy of decadent indulgence—as decadent as any upright Methodist can become," she noted wryly. In March, she became a campus social reformer, launching all sorts of activities, and finally in April, she tried on a "hippie" identity, complete with a painted flower on her arm.

"Aside from the basic spiritual side, Hillary was intrigued by trying to find illumination and insight into life through reading the Bible and other Christian literature," Jones said. As Hillary explained years later: "Thinking about Scripture and tradition and reason and experience really helps me order a lot of thought about faith and religion."

Some of that came from a required sophomore year course on the Old and New Testaments, which, in response to student agitation, later was dropped. It helped put "things into context," she said of the course taught by Clifford Green, a young Australian who later became a professor of theology and ethics at Hartford Seminary. "In addition to it being an academic exer-cise," said Green, "I think it gave students an opportu-nity to think through on a more adult level the religious beliefs they had brought with them from their childhood and youth."

Characteristically, Wellesley students did not pa-rade those religious beliefs. That was true of Hillary, who "didn't make a splash about her religious convictions though they were very much a part of her identity and motivated her outlook and her willingness to make commitments," recalled the Reverend H. Paul Santmire, Wellesley's first chaplain. He had been hired, in part, to reassure alumnae that despite its abolition of the sophomore Bible course, the college was as serious about religion as it had ever been. "This was a profoundly Protestant school that was so part of the leading Protestant culture of the country that it didn't even know it," said Santmire.

It was in her correspondence with Don Jones that Hillary discussed Reinhold Niebuhr, the leading Protestant scholar who was among the founders of Americans for Democratic Action and more thoroughly than any other twentieth-century American theologian discussed the proper relationship of religion and politics. At one point, she puzzled over whether Niebuhr was a conservative or liberal or, as Jones put it, "whether it was possible to be a realist about social existence and at the same time struggle for justice and reform? Did you have to be either conservative status quo or liberal idealistic?" Or, as Hillary herself wrote: "I wonder if it's possible to be a mental conservative and a heart liberal?"

Niebuhr contended that "religious faith is basically a trust that life, however difficult and strange, has ultimate meaning." And he argued that "individuals are never as immoral as the social situations in which they are involved" because individuals have "sensitivity to the needs of others." Thus, he concluded, institutions were more prone to unrestrained egotism and brute conduct than individuals even though it was the self-centeredness of individuals that infused their institutions with the same malady.

What political realists like Vice President Hubert Humphrey liked about Niebuhr was "the realism with which he viewed the human condition." So, the theology Hillary was absorbing in the 1960s was this kind of neo-orthodoxy, which was a revolt against Protestant "sentimental liberalism," said Jones. If there was a pragmatic side to Hillary, and Jones would ultimately position her somewhere between traditionalism and progressivism, it may have had "something to do with her Christian faith and her sense of human frailty—the irrationalities of human beings and hence the impossibility of envisioning a perfect world—and also with the difficulties of achieving justice and even the necessities of using power."

She objected to the Black Power extremism of Stokely Carmichael and his Student Nonviolent Coordinating Committee (SNCC). The summer before her sophomore year, rioting had ripped apart Chicago's West Side in the aftermath of Martin Luther King's demands for "a just and open city." "She really had a sense of what the civil rights movement meant and had some convictions about that herself, being favorably disposed to the major goals," said Jones. She wrote to him that fall that "Just because a person cannot approve of SNCC's attitude toward civil disobedience does not mean that one wishes to maintain the racial status quo."

Jones recalled that she talked about shifting her political views to the left. In her letters there was "a strong intellectual content and also self-reflection. We were beginning to engage in political discussions. She was coming out of her conservative ideology that she grew up with. In one letter, she talked about how pleased she was that liberal Republican John Lindsay won the mayoral election in New York."

She was a "wonk" long before the term was popularly identified with those who thrive on discussions about political issues. As a freshman, she started dating a Harvard student, Geoffrey Shields, also from Illinois. One of Shields's roommates was a black student with whom she often discussed integration. "The time when she seemed to lighten up the most was when there was a good, interesting, heated debate about issues, particularly issues that had a practical impact on the world—racial issues, the Vietnam War, civil rights, civil liberties," Shields told *The Boston Globe.*

She was a voracious newspaper reader. Over breakfast, she and friends often were so absorbed in debating issues that the Stone-Davis dining hall would be empty by the time they left. Theirs was not "gossip about boys," classmate Betsy Griffith told the *Globe,* "but about ways 'to solve the problems of the world.' "

Like others in her class, Hillary came to believe that "to minister" had a larger connotation than serving. "We were really trying to redefine Wellesley's motto, that we had a public role in life to do things for people," said Francille Wilson. "In the context of the 1960s, to do things for people meant different things. It is a way to understand Hillary."

For Hillary at that time, doing things for people meant those within her immediate world where she could make a difference. "There were a lot of issues, causes and movements during that period, and all kinds of people who never gave much, would jump on any bus going by, but she was far more thoughtful, always reading, thinking and talking, committing herself to action," said classmate Nancy Gist.

Hillary saw her role at college as trying to improve the system, a recurring pattern of how she operated and part of what she would later explain was a friend's "Bloom-where-you're-planted" philosophy. So she took on committee chores, working to eliminate irrelevant courses, increase black enrollment and faculty and relax parietal restrictions. Displaying an instinctive political maturity rare for her age, she became known as a coalition builder. "She had a way of being able to speak for all of us," said Wilson. "Just about everybody had been president of something in high school. There were many avenues to be a campus leader or activist. So not a lot of people were feeling that Hillary stole their thunder; maybe it was like being first among equals."

Not everybody felt comfortable around her. Among the campus "cools," "jerks" and "ughs," she was a "cool." Her friends were similarly self-confident and self-assured. "If you were somebody from Scarsdale High School, I'm sure you found it easier to be around her than if you were from someplace like Enid, Oklahoma," said a classmate. "It could be very intimidating."

She could be cold, aloof, cuttingly impatient at times—friends knew she "did not suffer fools," in the backhanded compliment routinely applied to bright and demanding people. "Not always easy to deal with if you were disagreeing with her," Ruth Adams, then-president of Wellesley, told *The Boston Globe*. "She could be very insistent." But she was also remembered as a person whose "glass was always half full, who always looked on the positive side."

If the 1960s was a defining decade, with nothing that would come later paralleling such dramatic change, 1968 was to be the defining year in Hillary Rodham's undergraduate life. It was a unique year that came at a moment when she was supremely attuned to the changes in the world and intellectually able to absorb them. The sexual revolution was getting under way that year when William Masters and Virginia Johnson's *Human Sexual Response* rejected tired old myths about female sexuality. It sparked a national debate, particularly in college dormitories around the country where young women discussed their right to sexual freedom.

The year also marked the ascendance of the Warren Supreme Court and, in a seminar on federal policymaking with political science professor Alan Schechter, Hillary was a spirited participant in discussions about the intellectual influence of that "liberal" court and the political activists of the time. "There was very little writing from a conservative perspective worth reading that was serious," said Schechter. "I would have students read Barry Goldwater's *Conscience of a Conservative*. Unlike twenty years later when intellectually fascinating conservative writings flourished, Goldwater's book was just too simpleminded and didn't focus on the major political problems of the era. Hillary read the book and must have made the connection that the

Goldwater responses to the political dilemmas confronting the nation were excessively simplistic."

Hillary's Goldwater Republican views already had turned left by way of the party's moderate Lindsay wing. And by 1968, in next-door New Hampshire, she and a brigade of Wellesley students began working as Eugene McCarthy liberals in his presidential primary campaign. "Looking at what was happening in the outside world, a lot of students active outwardly were active inwardly as well," said Stephen London. "Here were Hillary and other students in a society undergoing dramatic change during two very significant years in terms of social history. She, like so many students of that era, was going through a consciousness raising and becoming even more concerned, more radicalized with social issues."

Some activist Wellesley women, Hillary on occasion among them, headed for Cambridge, New Haven or New York to march for civil rights or against the war in Southeast Asia. That spring, a number of them joined the townspeople of Wellesley in a protest march organized by local ministers. When they applied for a permit to demonstrate, word leaked out to several veterans organizations. "We were threatened that we'd have our heads beaten in if we did," recalled the Reverend Landon Lindsay, assigned by his bishop two years earlier to be "the conscience" of the Wellesley Methodist church ("I lasted two years," he said).

The Tet offensive in late January 1968 had dealt a death blow to Lyndon Johnson's credibility. In mid-March, McCarthy nearly defeated him in the New

Hampshire primary. A few days later, Robert Kennedy tossed his hat in the ring for the Democratic presidential nomination. "So many students were tearing their hair out," said Schechter. "It was an era when you walked into a dorm at Wellesley and the smell of pot smoke would just confront you. The country had such godawful problems."

Then on April 4, 1968, word of the assassination of Martin Luther King swept across campus. Some students already had left for spring break. Hillary had not. Her roommate, Johanna Branson, was in their suite. "Suddenly the door flew open. Her bookbag flew across the room and slammed into the wall. She was distraught. She was yelling. She kept asking questions. She said, 'I can't stand it anymore. I can't take it.' She was crying," Branson told Charles Kenney of *The Boston Globe*. Hillary recalled, in an address at Wellesley in 1992: "My friends and I put on black armbands and went into Boston to march in anger and pain, feeling as many of you did after the acquittals in the Rodney King case."

There was no collective response on campus to King's murder until the following month. Members of Ethos, banding together as the May 8 Committee, threatened to call a hunger strike outside President Adams's office if she and the college did not finally address their demands. Rumors abounded about a faculty member's remark that the college wanted more black students but found it difficult when so many were from homes where the only literature they had to read were comic books. That proved to be a mobilizing jolt that, as one classmate put it, "set everybody on their ear."

"Clearly, it was the first form of activism at the campus," said Stephen London. "I remember Hillary very vividly being supportive, really relating to that, going through, as a lot of kids were, a real understanding of what it meant to be of color in American society. What happened on campus did nothing but underscore that. All of a sudden, people said, 'We never realized what problems existed here on campus.' Ethos provided an invaluable education experience for the white kids on campus."

Hillary had realized it sooner than most. Shortly after arriving as a freshman, she had taken a black student to church in the town of Wellesley one Sunday. Don Jones said people she later told in Park Ridge "thought she did this not out of goodwill, but as a symbolic gesture to a lily-white church." But in a letter she wrote to Jones about it, she said "I was testing me as much as I was testing the church" and that a year earlier, had she seen someone else do it, she might have thought: "Look how liberal that girl is trying to be going to church with a Negro."

After King's death, a meeting in the college chapel quickly deteriorated into a shouting match between angry students venting their frustrations over a variety of grievances. "The potential was definitely there—where you'd shut the campus down and go on strike against classes and have kind of typical-for-the-times student activism responses," Kris Rogers said. "So we turned to Hillary and asked if she wanted to have a role in trying to field the questions." She was quite masterful about it, making it clear that these were adults the college was dealing with and seeing to it that the issues under debate be addressed "within the academic context."

When Marshall Goldman, professor of Russian economics, implored students to "give up the weekends, something we enjoy. Don't give up classes— that's not sacrifice," Hillary was quick to respond, according to *The Wellesley News.* "I'll give up my date Saturday night, Mr. Goldman, but I don't think that's the point. Individual consciences are fine, but individual consciences have to be made manifest."

A campus teach-in to inform students through workshops rather than in classrooms about the meaning of King's death did not meet Hillary's expectations. "Although I respect the right of the student not to strike her classes, I was disappointed that there were not more people participating in the day's activities," *The Wellesley News* quoted her as saying. "I didn't learn anything new as far as the specific issues were concerned, although I did pick up some ideas."

It had been a propitious time for these young women to enter college. Opportunities were opening up to them that had not existed a few years earlier. Like many of her classmates, Hillary had arrived believing women could do the things men could do and that gender should not limit their ability to achieve. Instructors like Stephen London helped them make the connection between the events in the society around them and their own lives. "The civil rights movement had planted the seeds of the women's movement, and in some ways it was almost inevitable that we would look at other examples of inequality, one of which was how we could be treating women in such a discriminatory fashion as well," said London.

Still, in the shelter of all-female Wellesley, students didn't spend a lot of time arguing about women's rights. "We were living feminism in the sense that we were encouraged to be smart and do things," said Francille Wilson. "It would be later, out in the world, that we would discover that everybody didn't think it was wonderful to be smart, intellectually curious women."

Realizing that she could be more effective in her own milieu than agitating for change elsewhere, Hillary, the realist, set her sights on student politics as a way of bringing this tradition-bound institution into the twentieth century. In her sophomore year, classmates elected her their representative to student government. As a junior, she chaired the prestigious Vil Junior cadre, a select group of students who looked after entering freshmen, adding another constituency to her support base. Then at the end of her junior year, she ran for president of the student government.

In an hour-long debate at *The Wellesley News*, she and two opponents vied for an editorial endorsement that never came. The newspaper wrote: "They each expressed a desire for greater student jurisdiction in social matters and a more responsible role in academic decision making, but all three were equally vague as to exactly how they would implement the change in the power structure to achieve the second objective."

To what seemed her genuine surprise, Hillary

won the election. Showing up in Stephen London's class, she asked to speak to him. "The way she said it, I thought something had happened because she wanted to speak to me privately. 'I can't believe it,' she told me. 'I just was notified that I was elected student government president!' "

If that was a prospect that took getting used to, she had a summer to adjust. Fittingly, perhaps, she got a look at how big government operated when she went to work that June for the House Republican Conference in Washington. Schechter and a faculty committee chose her and thirteen other students for the Wellesley Internship Program, begun in World War II when the fuel shortage forced the college to add a winter vacation to its academic year. Competition had been keen. Like Hillary, most of the students chosen were political science majors with a strong interest in public law and politics. It was up to them to apply for the available internships on Capitol Hill and in the various government agencies.

Hillary arrived in Washington to find a city devastated by the assassination of Robert Kennedy. Out of three hundred applicants, she had been one of thirty hired by the GOP group. "We picked these people on the basis of their ability and what we thought they could contribute," said Melvin Laird, the then-congressman from Wisconsin who chaired the conference. "We never asked them—maybe we should have—for party affiliation although I tried to tell them why it was important to be a Republican. All these young people were activists—they wouldn't have applied if they weren't."

Laird paid his interns, in effect, by passing the hat among various Republican members of Congress, who then assigned the interns to their staffs for two months. He put Hillary on the payroll of Illinois Congressman Harold Collier, whose district included Park Ridge. "You'd go up and say, 'I've got a bright young constituent from your district.' He was very cooperative," Laird said. "That's how I got him to go along."

She was not just bright. "She presented her viewpoints very forcibly, always had ideas, always defended what she had in mind," said Laird. The conference staff was working up plans on revenue sharing that summer and also preparing a white paper on what Laird called the "fight-now-pay-later" way the Vietnam War was being financed. "We thought they [the Johnson administration] should come to Congress and get funding and that they'd gone beyond the congressional mandate of the Tonkin Gulf resolution."

Hillary wrote several papers for the conference, including one on revenue sharing. "She was for it," said Laird. "Instead of the categorical fixed grants being dictated on how you spent every dollar, she felt it was better to return funds to the states and local communities where the decision could best be made."

She was also outspoken on the war and left no doubt about her sentiments in spirited discussions with Laird, later to become secretary of defense in the Nixon administration, and others on the staff. Among them were three men who one day would head major Washington think tanks of more or less conservative intentions: David Abshire at the Center for Strategic and International Studies, William Baroody at the American Enterprise Institute and Edwin Feulner at the Heritage Foundation. "They were challenging people and would challenge these young people," said Laird. "They had great arguments and great debates. We wanted that."

That summer was significant for another reason: The national political conventions. The question among Hillary's liberal and independent-minded contemporaries was who to vote for in their first presidential election, although Hillary would learn that for her the question was moot. She would turn twenty-one on October 26 but because the state of Illinois cut off registration thirty days before an election, she would not be eligible to vote. "I've always been kind of sorry I couldn't have voted for Humphrey," she told me in an interview in 1993.

With Robert Kennedy dead and Eugene McCarthy out of the race, Democrats were left with Hubert Humphrey, whose domestic liberalism was commendable but whose loyalty to Lyndon Johnson on Vietnam was troubling. Many of Kennedy's youthful supporters were attracted to Nelson Rockefeller, the Republican governor of New York whose "New Politics" offered a four-point program on Vietnam and stressed his approach to urban problems.

In early August, Hillary went to Miami to work in a draft-Rockefeller effort. When Richard Nixon carried off the nomination, she returned to Park Ridge where later in the month she and her high school chum Betsy Johnson Ebeling rode the train to Chicago to take in the Democratic National Convention. "We saw kids our age getting their heads beaten in. And the police were doing the beating," Ebeling told *The Washington Post*. "Hillary and I just looked at each other. We had had a wonderful childhood in Park Ridge, but we obviously hadn't gotten the whole story."

Before Hillary returned to Wellesley in September, she went to see Saul Alinsky, the guru of community organizers whose approach to social change was an emphasis on teaching people to help themselves but also confronting government and corporations to provide the necessary resources. Terms such as "empowerment" and "entitlement" were coming into use while Alinsky was turning words into deeds by bringing energetic graduates of elite schools to the ghetto to organize grassroots efforts to force an improvement in living standards.

Back at Wellesley that fall, Hillary led the student government association in negotiations with the faculty over greater control of nonacademic community life. As Ruth Adams told *The Boston Globe*: "She was liberal in her attitudes, but she was definitely not radical. She was, as a number of her generation were, interested in effecting change, but from within rather than outside the system. They were not a group that wanted to go out and riot and burn things. They wanted to go to law school, get good degrees and change from within."

Wellesley's stated goal the previous spring, to enroll twenty-five additional black students, had fallen short by twenty-four. (The following fall, 104 would be accepted and fifty-seven would be enrolled.) But there was some progress. One sign of that was a young Harvard graduate student brought in as "head of house." Patricia King resided at Stone-Davis, where Hillary lived, but was available to students from around the campus.

"It was a major shift in the system," recalled King. "The girls had revolted. They wanted people close to their own age. It was difficult for me because I was a young African-American trying to figure out what I was going to do—it was before the women's revolution took hold and I was really self-absorbed, really struggling."

Three students managed to "penetrate" her self-absorption: Nancy Gist, who would study law at Yale and later become assistant director of the Massachusetts State Public Counsel's Office; Betsy Griffith, who would be headmistress at Madeira School near Washington; and Hillary. "She was a no-nonsense, very serious person who got through to me because I could hold a conversation with her on some of the things— Vietnam, Martin Luther King and Bobby Kennedy— that I was concerned with that year," said King.

Beyond the racial implications, King also seemed the perfect student guardian for the age, following a self-imposed rule of not intruding, not creating privacy problems, not patrolling the hall and giving people space. The fact that she was there at all was a sign of how far Wellesley had come in meeting students' demands. While some of those at staid old Wellesley bit their stiff upper lips, King dealt with her charges as adults. "They had men in the rooms by then," said King, who would become a professor of law at Georgetown University. "And they could spend the night."

Hillary's fourth and final year not only focused on student government but on her senior thesis. Alan Schechter remembered discussions they had on prospective topics. She decided she would write on community action programs and local community organizations that tried to fight poverty. "It was quite clear that though she started out a conservative, her interests were in how to resolve social problems, not necessarily in big government or how to use government but more in the notion of poor people taking control of their own lives."

Schechter said he was critical of it. "The concept of poor people taking control of their lives struck me as overly simplistic—wonderful, sweet-sounding rhetoric we could all believe in and ascribe to—who could be opposed to it? It was the classic American apple pie approach but an approach that failed to take into account all the factors of the political system that made it so difficult for the poor to participate and so easy for others to co-opt and exploit the poor. It failed to take into account that you needed structure and leadership and organization programs."

After a year of studying and evaluating community programs, what Hillary finally wrote, according to Schechter, was that "organizing the poor for community actions to improve their own lives may have, in certain circumstances, short-term benefits for the poor but would never solve their major problems. You need much more than that. You need leadership, programs, constitutional doctrines."

Hillary was also talking about law school, whether she should go to Harvard or Yale—if she could get in. "All during my growing-up years I had a combined message of personal opportunity but also public responsibility—that there were obligations that people who were as lucky as I was owed society," she said later. She had thought a little about "doing something in the area of organizing" similar to Saul Alinsky, she told *The Chicago Daily News* the summer she graduated. His view that deliberate agitations were the most effective way to force social change was a "good point," as was his notion that the middle class— "the kind of people I grew up with in Park Ridge"— was disaffected by confrontational tactics.

She had admired his courage but hadn't been sure of his "tactics" and didn't buy into his "whole theory," she told me in an interview. When he had offered her a job as an organizer with considerable responsibility after she graduated from Wellesley, she told him she was going to law school at Yale. "I remember him saying, 'Well, that's no way to change anything.' And I said, 'Well, I see a different way than you. And I think there is a real opportunity.'"

But her deeper interest lay in government institutions and how they related to one another. It was Schechter's opinion that after analyzing participation of the poor and Alinsky-style methods, she decided she could do more to help the poor by becoming a lawyer and by using the legal system for the purpose of stimulating change.

"We came to the conclusion that given what her interests were, Yale was the logical place," said Schechter. "It was much less oriented to teaching you how to be a successful money-earner as a lawyer and much more toward the philosophy and doctrines of law."

She had been leaning toward Yale but, just to be sure, she visited the Harvard Law School where a friend introduced her to a distinguished professor, telling him she was trying to decide whether to go there the following year or to "our closest competitor." As Hillary later recalled in an interview with *The Arkansas Democrat-Gazette*, "This tall, rather imposing professor, sort of like a character from *The Paper Chase*, looked down at me and said, 'Well, first of all, we don't have any close competitors. Secondly, we don't need any more women.' That's what made my decision . . . that fellow's comments iced the cake."

The letter Schechter wrote in October 1968 recommending that Hillary be admitted to Yale Law School was glowing, though, as time would prove, not at all exaggerated: "I have high hopes for Hillary and for her future. She has the intellectual ability, personality, and character to make a remarkable contribution to American society."

Hillary viewed that future as a pragmatic idealist. "I'm not interested in corporate law," she said. "My life is too short to spend it making money for some big anonymous firm."

Wellesley President Ruth Adams ruled out the idea almost immediately when a group of students approached her a few days before commencement to ask that someone from their own ranks be chosen to address the Class of 1969. As was tradition, the college administration had acted unilaterally when it invited

Senator Edward Brooke, the same moderate Republican Hillary and other campus Republicans had supported three years earlier, to give the keynote commencement speech. Wellesley had never had a student speaker on the commencement program and would not start then, replied Adams, all but showing the students the door. Eleanor Acheson and others in the ad hoc effort were disappointed but also undaunted. Their minds were made up: they would stage a counter-commencement and ask Hillary to speak.

As Hillary remembered events years later to sister alumna Marian Burros, by then a writer for *The New York Times*: "I said, 'I'll speak but I'm not going to speak at a counter-graduation. Let me go speak to Ruth Adams.' She was my friend. She was crusty and outspoken but I'd met with her once a week throughout the year." In their meeting, Hillary came to the point quickly. "I said, 'What is the real objection?' She said 'It's never been done.' I said, 'Well, we could give it a try.' She said, 'We don't know who they are going to ask to speak.' I said, 'Well, they asked me to speak.' She said, 'Well, I'll think about it.' "

Adams's eventual approval sent Hillary and her classmates into a frenetic marathon of gathering ideas. "I think they made the decision to let me speak on Wednesday or Thursday—very late before the Saturday commencement," she said. "So all my friends were jamming paper under the door [with notes like] 'Save it,' 'Here's my favorite quote'—I had friends writing poems. It was just this huge synthesis of everybody's thoughts—we were all on the same wavelength. I sort of put it all together."

The final version of the speech was a combination of prepared remarks—including a poem by classmate Nancy Scheibner, who contributed the oft-quoted phrase "The art of making possible"—and Hillary's own extemporaneous response to Brooke. She would later characterize Brooke's speech as "a defense of Richard Nixon . . . a pro forma commencement speech— you know, 'The world awaits you, we've got great leadership, America is strong abroad.'"

In Hillary's view, Brooke had addressed none of the realities Americans were struggling with and she had been both outraged and insulted. "We'd had assassinations. We were in the midst of a war everybody was confused about and most people didn't like," she said. "Civil rights, you know, all the great issues of the day were just kind of subsumed in this onward and upward" account of Brooke's.

Some of her classmates remembered that she spoke without notes for nearly ten minutes before picking up the text she and her friends had drafted. Nowhere in that version, released by Wellesley College, did the word "Vietnam" appear, although Brooke said later he remembered a reference she made to it. He opposed violent protest and was particularly critical of groups like Students for a Democratic Society, which he felt gave false optimism to North Vietnamese leader Ho Chi Minh about the extent of divisiveness among the American public. What Brooke had urged graduates to reject was "coercive protest. . . . So long as society retains a capacity for nonviolent political change, resort to political action is anathema."

Responded Hillary: "Every protest, every dissent,

whether it's an individual academic paper, [or a] Founder's parking lot demonstration, is unabashedly an attempt to forge an identity in this particular age. That attempt at forging for many of us over the past four years has meant coming to terms with our humanness." And further on, she said, "There's a very strange conservative strain that goes through a lot of New Left, collegiate protests that I find very intriguing because it harkens back to a lot of the old virtues, to the fulfillment of original ideas."

*Washington Post* reporter Judith Martin, describing Hillary's speech as "a mild rebuttal," wrote that if the speech had been given at Harvard, it would have "invited a mass walkout. . . . Reaction to her talk from the alumnae was in the order in which they sat—mostly silence to 1954; applause from there to mid-1959 and standing applause from mid-1959 through 1964, in the back."

In the front, the cap-and-gowned graduates of 1969 rose to their feet en masse and for seven minutes cheered this small, bespectacled classmate of theirs who had made Wellesley history before their eyes. Some relatives and faculty in the crowd of two thousand seemed shocked at such impertinence.

Senator Brooke, on the other hand, registered a generous smile and rated the speech "very charitable." Years later he said he remembered "several people coming up to me afterward saying something about her being rude. I didn't find her rude at all. I didn't disagree with a lot she was saying. It didn't hurt me that she said those things. She was speaking as a student and I was speaking as a United States senator. We were coming from different perspectives."

Dean Acheson, on occasion an unexpected defender of Richard Nixon's since he became president earlier that year, betrayed no shock, either. He was in the audience to see his granddaughter graduate. "One of the nicest things to happen so far," Hillary told reporters later, "is a note I received from Secretary Acheson, asking for a text of my speech."

For Francille Wilson, later to become assistant professor of African-American studies at the University of Maryland, Hillary's speech signified a coming of age at last for Wellesley. "When we started Wellesley, it was a girls' school," she said. "When we left, it had become a women's college."

Or at least it had in the minds of its graduates. Some traditions, however, take longer to change. When *Wellesley College, 1875–1975: A Century of Women*, the official history of the college, was published in 1975, there was no mention of Hillary Diane Rodham, her impact on the college or her history-making speech.

# 4

# Coming of Age at Yale

*"I began to think through a lot of the issues that affect children, both visible and invisible, and the role that the law can and cannot play."*

HILLARY RODHAM WAS no communal flower child in that dawning Age of Aquarius. But, when she arrived at Yale Law School in the fall of 1969, she found common ground with her fellow first-year students that quickly took root in determined, if peaceful, activism.

Within days, the quadrangle sprouted Buckminster Fuller—type domes and tents, pitched there for a week-long teach-in. Guest speakers held forth on the day's litany of issues. They ranged from poverty around New Haven and the war in Vietnam to the Chicago indictments charging radicals, including leaders of the Black Panther Party and Students for a Democratic Society, with conspiring to start a riot at the 1968 Democratic National Convention. There was so much

to shout down that student organizers decided everybody could learn more in the courtyard than the classroom those early autumn days.

And while the issues were intense, the mood was
loose. At one point author Ken Kesey brought his antic
Hog Farm on his painted bus all the way from Eugene,
Oregon, and another time a group called the Sunshine
Commune came up from Texas. The new term started
off with a rollicking, round-the-clock, set-to-music
reunion of old and new students. The teach-in, with
daily noon presentations from the stage, turned into a
love-in at the slightest excuse. When word got around
that J. William Moore, a law school icon whose works
on civil procedure were in every lawyer's library, was
about to turn sixty-four, he became the object of everybody's affection. Students serenaded him with the
Beatles's "When I'm 64," and "J. Willie" nailed down
his immortality by dancing onto the stage. Light shows
and music that went on all night lent a carnival air.

Not that all was carefree, the times being what
they were. Behind all the revelry, students kept track
of the infiltrating presence of Big Brothers from the
New Haven office of the Federal Bureau of Investigation. "FBI agents always kept their shoes shined,"
remembered Kris Olson Rogers, Hillary's Wellesley
classmate also studying law.

The two were among thirty women entering with
the Class of 1972, a tiny presence that was large only
in comparison to the classes preceding them. They
were unique because of their numbers, but not for
much else as they quickly discovered when they encountered the predictable surplus of academic arro-

gance. Among the more quotable bon mots was that of constitutional law professor Eugene Rostow, recently returned from Washington where he had been Lyndon Johnson's under secretary of state for political affairs. Yale was a place, he liked to remind listeners, where you could hear the clink of Phi Beta Kappa keys all the way to the post office.

Women's issues were laughable in some quarters although Yale President Kingman Brewster made an effort to involve women in decisions affecting students. Kris Rogers, later to become associate dean and professor of law at Northwestern School of Law of Lewis and Clark College, sat on selection committees to find a successor to Law School Dean Louis S. Pollak. Even so, a few of Hillary's law school sisters endured in silence the condescension of male classmates and faculty who seriously doubted that a woman's place was before the bench. Hillary, who had lived and played among brothers and boyfriends all her life and been assured she was as good as any of them, suffered no such intimidation.

"Some women were insecure about being there and very hung up about women in law school. There were a lot of people who were Northeastern cynical types either involved in identity crises or had a sense of cynicism or fatalism about the larger world. And while there were other women committed to public service, Hillary just stood out as someone who was marching forward," said Patricia Coffin Fry, another Wellesley classmate studying law.

A Vida Dutton Scudder Fellowship recipient from Wellesley, Hillary lived off campus in a two hundred unit high rise in downtown New Haven where she was remembered for her agreeable manner, if not necessarily her housekeeping. Hillary's commencement speech at Wellesley had won her widespread attention and that fall she was named to the League of Women Voters' Youth Advisory Committee. Periodically, she and other notable young women from colleges around the country met in Washington to draft ways of channeling youthful unrest toward more meaningful goals. One, they decided, was winning the vote for eighteen-year-olds. The chairman of the committee—and in the vernacular of the time, the only member over the age of thirty any of them would trust—was Peter Edelman, former legislative assistant to Robert Kennedy. He was also the husband of Marian Wright Edelman, the noted civil rights lawyer and advocate for disadvantaged children. In time, both Edelmans would be among a growing and loyal circle of Hillary's friends active in law, civil rights and the Democratic Party who would leave their imprint on government.

By the second semester, it was apparent that Hillary was a woman to watch at Yale. In the law school dining hall, as she had at Wellesley, she was the magnet. The times were "difficult and turbulent," she said. "There was a lot of confusion in our minds. Many arguments took place over food and drink and books in and out of the halls of the law school over what direction our country was heading. A lot of passion, a lot of concern. And what I remember most during that time is the seriousness with which all of us—students and professors—took the challenges that confronted our country."

Describing a New Haven restless with civil disturbance and a law school whose "physical well-being" was under challenge, she told law school alumni in 1992 of feeling profoundly distressed one day as she sat on a wall outside the school "just wondering what was to become of our school, and our country." Then one of her professors stopped to talk, telling her that "bad things happen in every society" but that "you cannot be discouraged. You have to keep trying."

With April had come the deluge. Black Panther Bobby Seale and seven co-defendants awaited trial in New Haven on charges of kidnapping and murdering a fellow Panther the previous spring. Echoing around the country were calls to students to descend upon the city for a May Day demonstration that would demand the trial be stopped and the accused freed.

President Brewster had fanned some of the flames when he voiced skepticism that black revolutionaries could get a fair trial anywhere in the country, and, backed by the faculty, had voted to "countenance" the strike.

Recalling the events in an article for *The New Republic*, Professor Alexander M. Bickel noted that "the law school—training still tells a little—was virtually untouched" by the furor over an untried indictment. Such was not the case with Yale's undergraduate and graduate students, who had "whipped themselves to a pitch of hysteria" over what he believed to be "a trumped-up crisis."

Whatever the intellectual ferment, merchants reflected the more pragmatic realities and boarded up store windows as the National Guard was called in. "It looked as if things might come apart," said law school dean Louis H. Pollak. "But Brewster had the extraordinary insight of saying, 'Well, the thing we've got to do is open up our dormitories and give those students places to eat.' That sort of took the wind out of the revolution."

Hillary and fellow students in First Amendment scholar Thomas Emerson's class attended court proceedings of the Panthers' cases, some as independent studies, others wholly extracurricular as part of Emerson's efforts to assist the American Civil Liberties Union. Hillary's job was to organize shifts for her classmates and make certain no proceeding went unmonitored. "We were supposed to be monitoring civil rights abuses as they occurred throughout the trial, then we would write papers on them, discuss them in the class and do reports for the ACLU," Kris Rogers said. It meant going in and out of the Black Panther headquarters to obtain documentation and other information. "It was pretty obvious that we were being surveilled by the FBI. I remember people parked in cars across the street. And I remember Emerson filing Freedom of Information Act requests to find out what photographs were being taken of his students."

That was the spring that Hillary, an unlikely Portia clad in blue-denim bell-bottoms and a chambray shirt, presided over a fractious ad hoc assemblage of students. Sitting calmly on a table in front of the crowd, she played the interpreter, the distiller, a role she would assume often in the years to come.

"She tried to make sure all the positions were clarified," said Kris Rogers, who was "far more to the left, and I remember trying to push her in that direction—she was the source of some of my frustrations." Hillary would have none of it. The way she followed Robert's Rules of Order was to strip a speaker's remarks to the bare essentials, moving back and forth between opposing sides. "Nowadays," said Rogers, "you'd call it international summitry."

It turned out that the greatest calming event for the law school was the most violent. A fire in the International Law Library one night had jolted students and faculty alike. "The great fear after the event— indeed, terror at the notion," said Pollak, "was that anybody could have deliberately set a fire, because whatever happens books can't be burned." Neither Yale nor the fire marshal was ever able to establish that it had been arson, though students were never convinced. "You can generate fantasies and put a name to it and none of it had any logic," said Pollak, himself under criticism for what some considered a tepid response to the Panther case.

Once the flames were extinguished by a student bucket brigade, everybody reassembled in the school's largest classroom to organize a round-the-clock security patrol of all the law school facilities for the balance of the year. However they felt about the Bobby Seale case or a student strike, setting fire to the books was "where we drew the line," said Kris Rogers.

For Pollak, the outpouring of support, he said later, had been "one of the most gratifying" experiences of his years at Yale. In the weeks that followed, part of that support was due to Hillary Rodham, who could speak to him, as one classmate told *Legal Times* in

1992, in a way that nobody else could. "She was some-how able to transmit the message without getting con-frontational or hysterical." The lesson Hillary drew from Pollak's leadership was that he had faced the crisis "with a stated commitment to the continuing role of the law, and how we had to view even disorder in a way that let us think of reasonable and legally oriented solutions."

To all of this, Richard Nixon added his comments about "these bums . . . blowing up campuses" being "the luckiest people in the world, going to the greatest universities, and here they are burning up the books, storming around about this issue. . . . Then out there, we have kids who are just doing their duty."

And then Nixon would up the ante in this genera-tional contest when, on April 29, 1970, he sent U.S. troops into Cambodia. Five days later, National Guardsmen opened fire on a crowd of antiwar demon-strators at Kent State University in Ohio, killing two protesters and two bystanders and wounding eleven. Calls for Nixon's impeachment went out from the Na-tional Student Association and within days thousands of students had arrived in Washington to demand that they be heard.

Hillary, again in black armband as she had been for Martin Luther King, Jr., was in Washington to address the fiftieth anniversary banquet of the League of Women Voters' National Convention. Hillary's Wellesley speech had won her national attention and launched her as a sought-after speaker. Through the years, her passionate and often stream-of-consciousness rhetoric sometimes got in the way of her racing intellect. This speech was notable not only for its fervent response to the immediate concerns—she implored her audience "to help stop the chain of broken promises" that had accompanied her to adulthood—but for the breadth of its vision, summing up the issues of the 1960s and projecting them into the next decade.

"Here we are on the other side of a decade that had begun with a plea for nobility and ended with the enshrinement of mediocrity," she said. "Our social indictment has broadened. Where once we advocated civil rights, now we advocate a realignment of political and economic power. Where once we exposed the quality of life in the world of the South and of the ghettos, now we condemn the quality of work in factories and corporations. Where once we assaulted the exploitation of man, now we decry the destruction of nature as well. . . ."

It was Hillary of Wellesley again, a twenty-two-year-old fresh-faced student reassuring yesterday's activists, women two and three times her age, that there were still ways to protest: "What kind of stock one owns. What do you do with your proxies? How much longer can we let corporations run us? Isn't it about time that they, as all the rest of our institutions, are held accountable to the people?"

Marian Wright Edelman keynoted that night. Pleading for a redefinition of what schools were supposed to be, she asked: "How in the world can we be confused about what's wrong with our children? What's wrong with our children is what's wrong with us. They have heard us talk about 'law and order' and they have seen us go out of our way to avoid desegregation. . . ."

For Hillary, sharing the dais with Edelman was a dream realized. Increasingly interested in the rights and development of children since high school, she had read about Edelman's work in a *Time* article the previous fall. Months later she saw on a bulletin board that Edelman was going to speak at Yale.

"After hearing her speak about her experiences as a civil rights lawyer, about her commitment to do what she could to use her Yale education on behalf of the poor, I went up to her and asked if I could work for her that summer," Hillary told law school alumni. "She told me I was welcome but she had no money to pay me. I asked her whether, if I could figure out how to be paid, I could work for her. Being a good Yale Law School graduate, [Edelman] said, 'Of course.' "

It was all the encouragement Hillary needed. "Meeting somebody like Marian, who had a passion about helping children and had a lot of the same values that I had, was a turning point in my life," she said.

So she went in search of funding and found it in a grant by the Law Student Civil Rights Research Council supporting students working in civil rights. Edelman was impressed by Hillary's persistence, interest in children's issues and determination to find enough money to live on. "I always liked people who could find ways to get things done," Edelman said. "She was one of those from the beginning."

Hillary went to work for Edelman that first time as an intern. It was ten years after the Edward R.

Murrow documentary about migrant workers in Florida, *Harvest of Shame.* "I just saw so much, such a great need, and felt that children often didn't have any voice speaking for them," Hillary said.

Edelman had steered her toward Senator Walter Mondale's subcommittee studying migratory labor. Mondale had worked closely with Edelman on the Child and Family Services Act, a major bill to provide compensatory education and day care in the earliest years of life. Mondale remembered "some really tough issues concerning the treatment of migrants—housing, health care, nutrition—and tough hearings" going on involving an orange juice concentrate plant in Florida where housing was especially grim.

"We had a real shootout," said Mondale. "Their lawyer was Joe Califano. I had a meeting with Joe and said that the only way they were going to come out of this alive was with a solid commitment about new housing and to support the National Labor Relations Act inclusion for migrant workers."

For Hillary, working with the Mondale subcommittee interviewing migrants had introduced her to "the conditions in migrant labor camps and to the problems posed by segregated academies that were fighting for tax-exempt status under the Nixon administration, and I came back to law school with a growing commitment toward children, and particularly poor children and disadvantaged ones."

Living on the law school campus, by then, in a suite she shared with a young woman from Burma, Kwan Kwan Wang, Hillary put together a program that permitted her to work at the Yale Child Study

Center. She audited classes at the medical school, and worked with the staff of the Yale New Haven Hospital on problems that were just emerging, among them child abuse, only then being identified as a serious issue.

She studied with psychologist Joe Goldstein, whose course on children and the law had been a "seminal" experience, as one friend put it, and with psychiatrist Jay Katz, whose interests in children's rights she shared. "Because of conversations with them, because of research that I was fortunate enough to do on a book Joe was writing with Anna Freud and Al Solnit," Hillary said, "I began to think through a lot of the issues that affect children, both visible and invisible, and the role that the law can and cannot play."

She was back and forth between New Haven and Washington often that fall, monitoring Capitol Hill hearings on children's issues. And she continued to look to Marian Wright Edelman as a mentor. But Hillary's life was not all books, hearings and long stays in the law school library, to which she reportedly had her own key. Wang said she was "very focused and serious about her studies but she was also easy to be around, down-to-earth, fun, endearing and caring. I call it Hillary's hippie stage when she wore big glasses and sloppy clothes. She had a wonderful raucous laugh."

Wang had come to Yale on a fellowship and dreaded her first winter outside the tropics. "I told Hillary I didn't know how I was going to survive the snow because I was sure it must be really cold. Then one evening when I was studying, she came knocking on the door and said, 'Come on out, come on out. Look, it's snowing. Let's get in the car'—she had a car at the time—'and I'll drive you around and show you the first snowfall. It's going to be very pretty.' I was so excited and it was so pretty, and when I said so, she said, 'Well, you better enjoy it now because tomorrow it's all going to be black slush!' And, of course, it was."

Men went in and out of Hillary's life. There had been someone in her freshman year, a carryover from Wellesley, and later someone she also saw in Washington. Then, in early 1971 he was displaced by a "sunny Southerner with Elvis sideburns."

Bill Clinton, an ever-charming but also worldly Southerner by way of Georgetown and Oxford universities, had arrived at Yale that fall. He lived off campus with three other law students in a Milford, Connecticut, beach house. He worked at three paying jobs to augment a scholarship and also in the Senate campaign of Joseph D. Duffey against Republican Lowell Weicker. Duffey lost and Bill Clinton turned his attention back to an academic life that eventually coincided with Hillary's in a course on political and civil liberties. She was aware of him just as Bill was aware of her but until events—read that fate—placed them both in the library one evening there had been no communication.

Jeffrey Gleckel said he had been studying when Bill came over to say hello. "Somehow we started talking about whether or not he should join the *Yale Law Journal*. I was trying to promote it by describing why he might want to join—that it was an excellent entrée if you were interested in a judicial clerkship, or in teaching in a law school. He was sort of listening, though very courteously. I had a sense that he was sort of skeptical, not so much about what I was saying as in the sense that maybe he wasn't that interested in being a law school professor or clerking for a federal judge."

Then, Gleckel recalled, "little by little, it seemed to me his concentration was disappearing. He listened but was saying much less. His glance began to wander and he seemed to be looking over my shoulder. I was trying to find a way to look in an inconspicuous manner and so I sort of turned around halfway as an excuse to scratch my leg or something and there I saw, seated nearby at a desk with a stack of books and notepads, Hillary Rodham, who also was an acquaintance."

From then on, Gleckel said, Bill's attention was negligible. "Finally, Hillary walked over and said something like 'Look, you've been staring at me for five minutes. The least you can do is introduce yourself.' Bill is not usually at a loss for words but he was almost flabbergasted. He didn't say, 'I'm Bill Clinton'; in fact, he didn't seem to know what to say. But when he did introduce himself, I realized right then that as far as the *Law Journal* was concerned it was a lost cause. I sort of politely excused myself."

Hillary told Kwan Kwan Wang about meeting Bill Clinton. "Not in a lot of detail other than that it's 'a change in our lives, that we're always meeting new people, that you never know when you meet another new person what's going to happen, that it's hard to make breaks and hard to break old ties.' She was dating that other person. I don't know if it was a serious relationship," said Wang.

Hillary later said that in the very first conversations she had with Bill, she was "so struck by how he was able to be so smart and so human, at the same time. I just never had met anybody like that. It was a unique combination, particularly in a place like Yale Law School where the kind of stresses and ambitions are all very focused, and Bill was just extraordinary in his interest in other people. His commitment to policies and the public interest just stood out."

Bill introduced Hillary to his roommates—or, as Douglas Eakeley characterized them, "his parents"— soon after. Eakeley, a friend from their Oxford days, Donald Pogue, who had been brought together with Bill through a mutual friend at Oxford, and William T. Coleman, III, whose father was secretary of transportation at the time, were already aware of Hillary.

"It's hard to describe the chemistry. We watched all the other young ladies disappear in a hurry when Hillary appeared on the scene," said Pogue. "Hillary had a sharp mind coupled with a traditional Midwestern openness. Bill was the quintessential Southerner, charming and gregarious. It was fun to watch the dance."

For Bill, who had just broken up with another young woman, the last thing he wanted was a romantic involvement even if Hillary was "the greatest thing on two legs," as he later described her to *Vanity Fair*'s Gail Sheehy. His future, he said he told her, lay in Arkansas. "It's just who I am." And hers—that is if she wanted it—was in public office. The attraction for each of them was powerful. "He wasn't afraid of me," said Hillary.

Friends saw them as perfectly suited, their differences complementing each other. In addition to their curious, lively intellects, their fascination with the role of law in public policy and their relish for debate, they were a lot of fun to be around.

That fall, they set up housekeeping in a sparsely furnished three-room apartment on the ground floor of a Federal-style frame house a short distance from campus. The dining table was early backyard—a picnic type—and the bed was generously described by a previous tenant as a platform model with "a huge hunk of foam rubber."

Their social life was freewheeling, with music, beer but mostly talk. Dinners were movable—even feasts when more adept cooks in the crowd, like Pogue, put together his then-famous coq au vin. He and Susan Bucknell eventually would marry, as would Kris Olson and Jeffrey Rogers, son of Nixon's secretary of state, William Rogers. "I still have this image of Bob Reich sitting on a three-legged stool that somebody had given us as a wedding gift," said Kris Rogers of the classmate President Clinton would one day name secretary of labor, "holding forth on some economic theory or other."

But social life was always a distant second to the business at hand for Hillary, which was beginning to come into focus as legal advocacy for children. Rather than trying to deal with grand policy, Hillary was learning about the issue one case at a time. Penn Rhodeen, an attorney with the New Haven Legal Assistance Association, said Hillary telephoned him one day in the fall of 1971 to ask about working together. "I was having big battles with the state welfare department, which then had jurisdiction over children in need of protection, children who couldn't live with their families. She said she heard I was giving them a pretty hard time."

What would impress Rhodeen was that Hillary, a rank amateur then on the subject of foster care, had arrived at pretty much the same conclusion he had as a lawyer. "If where a foster child is placed is working out, don't mess with it. If you ask an old grandma and a world expert what's important here, they say about the same thing. It's the whole middle level that's fighting over turf, saving face and often winding up with everything backward."

Together, Rhodeen and Rodham worked on a case involving a poor, older foster mother who had taken in a baby of Italian and African-American parentage and had cared for her about two years when the state decided she was free for adoption. "If you were designing the ideal family for this child at birth, it probably wouldn't look like that," said Rhodeen. "But the point was, once you started understanding the problem developmentally, you realized there was nothing worse that could happen to that child than to be taken out of that home."

Rhodeen said Hillary was "very much in tune with the fundamental moral dimension of the problem—that you should do these things because they were right and not simply to save a buck." Even Walter

Mondale, "the guy who was seen as the real champion of children's issues, to the extent anyone was," upset her at times when he couched arguments "in utilitarian terms, that it was cheaper this way or the choice was welfare or jail care."

Rhodeen said that the example they often used was that the courts were geared up in such a way that in commercial cases if there were a dispute over a carload of perishable fruit, almost certainly authorities would convene court on a Saturday.

"But an equally perishable child would be shoved to the back of the line," he and Hillary used to say. "People would be looking for all kinds of ways to get rid of the case, trying to force an appropriate compromise just to keep it out of the courthouse. What was lacking was the sense that time was ticking away in the kid. That time was the enemy in all kinds of ways that just wasn't in the system."

At Christmas that year, Hillary and Bill went their separate ways, though not for long. The day after Christmas, at home in Park Ridge, Hillary told her mother that a young man she had met at Yale was coming to spend a few days. The moment Dorothy Rodham opened the door she knew there was "an air of seriousness about him," she told *Paris Match*. "The introductions were rather cold. To tell the truth, I would have preferred that he left. He had come to take my daughter away!"

But while introductions were chilly—"Hello, my name is Bill Clinton," he said. "That's nice," Hillary's mother said she replied—she managed a certain graciousness, calling up to Hillary in her second-floor bedroom that Bill had arrived, then sending him up to see her. For the next week, he slept in seventeen-year-old Tony Rodham's room—"My husband and I watched that he did not leave it!"—and over the dinner table the Rodhams came to know some of the passion Hillary and Bill shared about their "humanist vision of America."

Dorothy Rodham had known nothing of Bill Clinton. Only on his second day there, as she sat in the living room reading a philosophy book, did she find out how brilliant he could be. When she told him she was taking a philosophy course, he launched into an impressive discussion about it. There had never been anyone at home she could talk to about the course, she said, "and from that moment, I loved him immediately."

Throughout that week, as Dorothy Rodham recalled, conversation went on for hours and came "from the heart. . . . Incessant, always the same subjects: Arkansas! American society! They never stopped thinking about it." One day she decided to ask what he intended to do after he finished college, thinking he would say something about joining a law firm in New York or Los Angeles. Her question had surprised him. He was going back to Arkansas, of course, to work for his state and its people. She remembered thinking that it was all well and good that he pursued his ideals, she was even pleased that he felt that way, "but my daughter"—whom she had secretly hoped might one day be the first woman on the Supreme Court—well. But Dorothy Rodham had not instilled in her daughter a sense of self-esteem so she could start telling her what to do now. Whatever they wanted to do with their lives didn't concern her. "Hillary was well prepared," she concluded, "and Bill was brilliant."

That winter, Hillary and Bill teamed up in a semester-long competition that culminated in a mock trial for the Barristers Union prize. Presided over by real judges, with real juries of New Haven residents returning the verdicts, the trials followed prescribed fact patterns. Among the Rodham-Clinton team's first victims as they worked their way through the rounds were Sidney H. Stein and Russell Bellavance. Hillary and Bill had come up with not just a "novel defense," said Stein, "but an ingenious one."

As the prize trial drew near, Hillary and Bill spent weeks of late-night sessions putting together their case, rehearsing arguments and preparing witnesses, among them Kris Rogers, who would portray a floozie of questionable credibility. The day of the trial, Doug Eakeley, one of the two runners-up, gave the Rodham-Clinton opening argument to the jury, then Bill and Hillary took over. Bill's courtroom style was a folksy display of talk-to-the-jury skills combined with a perceptive mind that could see points others would not. And Hillary, her legal homework down pat, went through a dazzling exhibition of shrewd arguments and intellectual defenses. The end result, said Don Pogue, was "a performance about as high-powered as you could expect, a delightful counterpoint between a combination of Bill's subtle charm and Hillary's sharp analysis."

Most of the memories about the trial would be forever hazy. Two, however, were not. One was that the presiding judge was Abe Fortas, the former Supreme Court associate justice whose nomination as chief justice in 1968 the Senate refused to consider. A few months later, under threat of possible impeachment proceedings because of conflict of interest and other charges, Fortas resigned from the court. His presence at Yale triggered a story, which may have been apocryphal. His portrait once had hung in the Yale Law Library but had mysteriously disappeared. When he returned to the school to preside at the trial, the portrait—equally mysteriously—reappeared.

The other memory is an undisputed fact: Hillary and Bill lost.

What Bill remembered about the trial was how proud he had been of Hillary. What others remembered was that when Hillary showed up, Bill predicted nobody would pay any attention to what she was saying, only to what she was wearing—a spectacularly vibrant orange dress.

A year and a half later, one visiting "judge" in that Barristers Union trial series, civil rights attorney John Doar, remembered her only too well. Burke Marshall, a teacher of Hillary's and an old friend of the judge's, had recommended her to Doar for a job. So had Bill Clinton, when he turned down a similar offer. Neither Marshall nor Clinton need have bothered. Doar had found Hillary's trial work impressive. "I'm sure that without Burke Marshall's recommendation," Doar told me, "I'd have hired her anyway."

The job, Hillary learned, was with a team of lawyers Doar was putting together in Washington.

They would have one assignment: to amass the evidence the House Judiciary Committee needed to conduct an impeachment inquiry. Depending upon their findings and what the committee recommended, the defendant would be that old nemesis of Hillary's generation—President Richard Milhous Nixon.

# 5

# *From*
# *Front Row*
# *to*
# *Center Stage*

*"We have a system that truly does work, if only*
*we become involved in it."*

THE POLITICAL SCANDAL that came to be called Watergate was at best a blip on the minds of anyone living outside of Washington in the summer of 1972 when Bill Clinton and Hillary Rodham went to Texas to help in George McGovern's campaign for president. State coordinators were Bill and writer Taylor Branch, later to win a Pulitzer Prize for *Parting the Waters: America in the King Years, 1954–63.* They had met three years earlier at a Martha's Vineyard retreat of young leaders trying to figure out whether the best way to work against the war was through election, legislation, by demonstrations or some combination.

In June, Hillary was sent to Texas by the Democratic National Committee to get out the vote, particularly among Hispanics in South Texas and newly enfranchised eighteen-year-olds. "You were driven by the fantasy that the election of a peace candidate would become close and turn on Texas and the marginal voters," Branch said. "If we didn't think that, I wouldn't have been there. And I don't think Hillary would have been there either."

Sara Ehrmann, a veteran McGovern legislative aide from Capitol Hill, met Hillary one day when she walked into McGovern headquarters in San Antonio. She remembered a "smart, tough, determined kid" in brown corduroy pants, a brown print shirt and tied-back hair. "Who's in charge here?" Hillary questioned with her characteristic directness.

"I told her I was in charge," said Ehrmann. "The more we talked the more I liked her. You couldn't spend five minutes with her without noticing her powerful focus and her drive. She had this raucous humor and incredible laugh—there was a total lack of pomposity."

Which was not quite what Ehrmann had expected of a campaign volunteer straight from the privileged enclave of an Ivy League campus. "You know these Yale kids, they thought they were going to save the world. I don't think Hillary ever thought that. She was a very pragmatic person."

Betsey Wright, a politically savvy Texan determined that more women should run for public office, first met Hillary in the McGovern campaign. Almost immediately, she put Hillary's name on her list of likely future women candidates where it stayed for about two years. "When she decided to marry this guy and move to Arkansas," Wright said later, "I knew running for office was highly unlikely."

When Hillary was not traveling around Texas, she shared a two-bedroom apartment in Austin with Bill and Taylor Branch. They also shared a growing sense of desperation. Even that summer, it was pretty apparent that nobody was going to save the world with McGovern. Aside from his pledge to end the war in Vietnam, the only other issue with a hope of igniting voter interest was a growing volume of puzzling questions related to the June 17 break-in of the Democratic National Committee headquarters in the Watergate office complex by men with sketchy ties to the U.S. government. The White House had denied any involvement but, not surprisingly, in the McGovern camp feelings ran high that somebody was lying.

"We knew that was a pretty fundamentally corrupt thing," recalled Branch, "not just in the sense of political corruption but in the kind of blue-collar burglar sense. There were guys wearing masks having to put their hands up, a criminal element that couldn't be papered over with policy language. We knew people were lying. We knew something was really wrong."

He and Bill talked a great deal about that and what effect the issue would have on that year's congressional races. If not then, at least by 1974, Bill fully intended to run for office once he had his law degree. He kept in touch with Senator J. William Fulbright and other Arkansas mentors about his possible options. One House race he thought about was in the Fayetteville area around the University of Arkansas, where Fulbright had once been president. The drawback was that it was a Republican stronghold whose congressman was the well-entrenched John Paul Hammerschmidt.

Elective politics did not hold the same allure for Hillary. Branch said that at the time, the two of them tended to view the grassroots courting of local pols as a necessary evil. "To me, working with elected officials was something you had to do to get the war ended, to change things," he said. "I think Hillary was a lot like me."

Even then around the apartment when she and Taylor Branch talked, she was "more focused on the grand cosmic questions" bothering people their age: morality—or lack of it—in the world, the alienation they felt, whether the system worked and what they could do to end the war. "In that sense," said Branch, "she was more typical of our generation than Bill was."

Bill Clinton saw the McGovern campaign, as he had Joe Duffey's Senate race two years earlier, as another field laboratory. He was the purest of political creatures who made no secret of his own ambitions: he intended to get himself elected to office, and soon. And, indeed, he was gifted at coddling county chairmen, massaging egos of low-rent politicians, working out accommodations that would get the most votes and making everybody smile. It fell to Taylor Branch to raise the money, pay the bills, do the firing. "Bill said that since everybody was mad at me anyway, it would be politic for me to do the firing because I didn't have any reputation to protect. I thought that was both shrewd and logical."

For all her interest in the issues and process of

politics, Hillary had nothing like Bill's fire in the belly to face voters. In those days she never expressed any personal interest in running for public office, though, according to Kristine Olson Rogers, friends "assumed she was going to run someday."

On the national scene, certainly prospects were dim for women in elective positions. Senator Margaret Chase Smith of Maine was about the extent of it. "When you said 'governor' or 'senator,' you thought male," said William Coleman, one of Bill's housemates at Yale. He and other Yale friends saw Hillary as smart and quick to grasp the issues but not "the flesh-to-flesh, hand-to-hand type Bill was. . . . Bill could hang out at the bowling alley," said Coleman. "I didn't see Hillary at too many bowling alleys."

Still, whatever their approaches, Bill and Hillary were both part of the hard-core campaign staff totally committed to McGovern and the antiwar cause. They were typical of both the intensity and the amateurishness of a campaign that provided a generation of political operatives with on-the-job training. But it was also notable for a variety of blunders best capsulized by the surprise announcement of McGovern's running mate, Missouri Senator Thomas Eagleton, that he had been under treatment for serious mental depression.

If McGovernites could be faulted for losing their focus, such was not the case with their dedication. They worked hard—eighteen-to-twenty-hour days. Some played even harder. Not Bill and Hillary, according to Garry Mauro, whose job was hitting college campuses to register eighteen-year-olds. "When we'd all sit around at Scholz [Bier Garten], they were intellectually engaged, totally focused on the campaign. I'd have a pitcher of beer in front of me and they'd have two Cokes."

Even romance—and Hillary and Bill's year-old liaison was still in what some called the "new love" stage—never overshadowed the reason she was in Texas. "She was definitely not somebody who was going to sit around for social reasons," said Branch. "I don't think she would have come down there with no job."

Meanwhile, the rumor mill churned endlessly, raising hopes that momentum would build once investigative reporters besides *The Washington Post*'s Bob Woodward and Carl Bernstein started breaking stories about Watergate. For weeks, the campaign staff talked about an exposé Walter Cronkite and CBS Television were preparing. The evidence CBS amassed was more forceful than anything else on TV but by the time the series hit the nation's living rooms, it was already too late. "I remember watching it in the Austin headquarters and wondering, 'Why doesn't this have an impact?'" said Mauro, later to become Texas land commissioner.

For those who had been tuned in to the antiwar movement and the general disaffection with those running American society, Watergate was the bleak crystallization of all their suspicions. Yes, there were sinister forces out there manipulating the system to their own ends. But no, no one seemed to care. Nixon hardly needed to campaign.

In Texas, the game was more a question of subtraction as former Democratic Governor John Connally, by then Nixon's treasury secretary, helped round up deserting Democrats. Lyndon Johnson, whose own pragmatic liberal accomplishments had been dashed on the shoals of the war, sat out the campaign on his ranch near Austin, long-haired and in weakening health. (One of Bill Clinton's notable successes was to arrange a lunch between LBJ and McGovern, resulting in a local newspaper story that could be construed as an endorsement.)

Watergate was widely perceived as a "third-rate burglary," as Nixon's press secretary characterized it. The real threat to the middle class, many believed, was George McGovern and his "new politics" of radical activists and minority groups preparing for takeover. As far as many voters seemed to feel, the tie-dyed, bell-bottomed army of McGovern volunteers were the problem, not the solution.

Bill and Hillary stayed through the election, and like others around them, watched the final agonizing hours of that devastating self-destruction. It didn't take long, however, for the pall it cast to lift. The next night, everybody pitched tents at the ridgetop ranch of Bob Armstrong, the Texas land commissioner whom President Clinton would name an assistant secretary of interior, and pretended they could see forever.

Back in New Haven, Hillary and Bill breezed through their semester exams, then went home for Christmas. She had stayed at Yale for an extra year of schooling, continuing to refine her expertise in child law issues by helping the staff at Yale New Haven Hospital create policies to deal with child abuse. And she studied child development theory at the Yale Child

Study Center—in particular the need for self-esteem among children growing up in poor families.

All Bill Clinton wanted to do after graduating in 1973 was return to Arkansas with law degree in hand. He told author Garry Wills for *Time*, "I thought I would hang out my shingle in Hot Springs and see if I could run for office." Of that part he was certain. What was not so certain was Hillary. Would she eventually come with him?

During a break from school, he and his mother talked about life without Hillary. In an interview at her home outside Hot Springs, Arkansas, in August 1992, Virginia Clinton Kelley described how the two of them talked about what lay ahead as they sat in his car before he set off for New Haven. "I'll never forget his words as long as I live," she told me. "He said, 'Mother, I want you to pray for me that it's Hillary because if it isn't Hillary, it's nobody.'"

"We were both very concerned about our country and its direction and fascinated by politics and committed to public service," Hillary told a Chautauqua, New York, audience in 1991. "We also realized that a marriage between two people like us was never, ever going to be easy, if it could even happen at all. When we graduated from law school, he went right back to Arkansas. I wanted nothing to do with that."

Instead of a shingle in Hot Springs, Bill ended up behind a lectern at the University of Arkansas in Fayetteville, teaching a course in criminal procedure. Still not ready for life in the Ozarks, Hillary joined a small staff Marian Wright Edelman had put together when she set up the Children's Defense Fund that year.

Working as the staff attorney, Hillary and others went door-to-door across the country comparing census data with school populations.

"We'd find these census tracks with all these children being reported but then when you'd look at the school population there would be this big discrepancy," she told writer Marian Burros. "We found children who were being kept out of school because they had mental or physical problems. Or we'd find children whose families were new immigrants and were afraid to send them to school. We'd find children who were too poor. I worked on juvenile justice problems. I traveled to different states and was involved in lawsuits about juvenile issues. That's what I cared about, what I wanted to do."

Then in the fall of 1973, Richard Nixon came back into Hillary Rodham's life. By October, not quite a year after Nixon's resounding victory with 60.8 percent of the popular vote, the denouement of his presidency had begun. He fired Archibald Cox, the special Watergate prosecutor whose subpoena of nine tape recordings of Nixon conversations had been upheld by the Court of Appeals. The media called it the Saturday Night Massacre; the public called it an outrage. Congressional offices were deluged with mail, most of it demanding at least an investigation. By December, members of the House Judiciary Committee had found the man to conduct it, a fifty-two-year-old Wisconsin Republican named John Doar who had headed the Justice Department's Civil Rights Division under Presidents Kennedy and Johnson.

This was the same Doar who in the early 1960s

strode up to bullhorns and fire hoses and faced the
bulldogs on the bridge at Selma, Alabama. If accused
of anything during his civil rights days, it was that he
wanted to go forward only with winnable cases. Putting together his impeachment inquiry staff of lawyers,
he had solicited recommendations from old civil rights
comrades such as Yale Law School's Burke Marshall.
He looked for thorough and impartial lawyers without
political axes to grind. They would have to do some
mighty legal grunt work, paging through much un-
charted legal territory on a tight deadline in what
promised to be one of the most sensitive congressional
investigations in history. For Hillary, it would be "one
of the great experiences professionally and politically
that I've ever had, to be involved with lawyers of that
caliber and that level of commitment to the country.
What a gift! I was twenty-six years old. I felt like I
was walking around with my mouth open all the time,"
she told me.

Wearing her ubiquitous blue jeans, big blue shirt
and studious-looking glasses, Hillary Rodham came on
staff in January 1974, one of three women among forty-
three lawyers handpicked by Doar. Their jobs were so
sought after that two staff assistants did nothing but
deal full-time with the hundreds of résumés coming in
from all over the country. And so, remarkably, the
young woman who had had a front-row seat in so many
of the dramas of the 1960s—from Martin Luther King,
Jr., in Chicago to the Democratic National Convention
to the Black Panther trial to the McGovern campaign,
which was the decade's final performance—was now at
center stage for the first act of the 1970s.

She came with a reputation as a no-nonsense student activist, which might have seemed at odds with Doar's insistence on impartiality. "I think he wanted us to come across as being neutral," said one of his lawyers. "On the other hand, he wanted people who were going to be absolutely devoted to the cause." If Doar had any concerns about Hillary's devotion, they evaporated, for she soon was among the inner circle. Doar had kind of a kitchen cabinet, and the longer she was there the higher her standing rose with the top people. "I don't think she did that by stepping on people's toes," said one staffer, "but because she was highly qualified." Said Doar: "I didn't single her out as outstanding. She was one of the team."

Among those who befriended her was Bernard Nussbaum, hired as a senior associate special counsel, and later Bill Clinton's White House counsel. Nussbaum often drove Hillary home to Sara Ehrmann's in the early hours of the morning. "So the kid wouldn't get attacked," said Nussbaum. "It wasn't the best part of southwest Washington," Ehrmann admitted.

Hillary's first assignment was to write all the procedural rules, an area of concern to Doar. Nobody knew anything about impeachment. There was information about what the Senate sergeant at arms proclaimed: "All persons are commanded to keep silent on pain of imprisonment while the House of Representatives is exhibiting to the Senate of the United States articles of impeachment against_____." And information about who sat where. But there was very little about the burden of proof and the rules of evidence. The last impeachment had been in 1936 and involved a federal judge. The only president to be impeached was Andrew Johnson in 1868 when he fired his secretary of war without notifying the Senate. When he was tried by the Senate for repudiating the Tenure of Office Act, he was acquitted by one vote. (Sixty years later, the Supreme Court ruled in a similar case that the act was unconstitutional.)

Dagmar Hamilton, who had taught government at the University of Texas and recently passed the Texas bar exam, recalled that Hillary "literally hit the ground running. She probably was asked the same questions in the same rather vague way some of us other lawyers were asked: 'See what you can find out about procedures.' " Hillary approached her assignment methodically, as usual. She made a chart. "It was done in a very lawyerly fashion," said Hamilton. "It showed initiative and her bright and analytical mind. I admired it. It was one of those good things you look at and say, 'I wish I'd thought of that.' "

The staff was divided into task forces dealing with Constitutional and legal research—"C and L" in office parlance—and three other areas such as criminal break-in, "plumbers" and emoluments. In addition to Hillary and Hamilton, there was Terry Kirkpatrick, a young lawyer from Arkansas who had been working for the Arkansas Supreme Court. Over dinner in Little Rock one night, Bill Clinton told Kirkpatrick and her husband, fellow lawyer Rafael Guzman, about turning down a job with Doar but that a friend of his had been hired. Did they know anybody who might be interested in going to work for Doar? "Did we!" said Kirkpatrick, an early beneficiary of the Bill Clinton network as one of the attorneys he hired after he became attorney general of Arkansas.

Hamilton was certain that their task force was the most interesting. She researched English impeachment cases, and Hillary examined American ones. "You didn't get stuck on the little pieces of milk fund or Cambodia," said Hamilton. "Our job was to look back at historical impeachment but also executive privilege. When the briefs were being filed seeking the tapes and when the articles of impeachment were being drafted, the C&L people were doing that. Within that framework, Bill Weld [later to become governor of Massachusetts] wrote a magnum opus on impoundment."

At another point Hillary and Fred H. Altshuler, a young lawyer from the West Coast, studied the White House staff under Nixon. "If you went through the chain of command," said Altshuler, who became one of the final editors of material being submitted to the committee, "it indicated that the president made key decisions himself, that they were not something he delegated to underlings. Seeing who reported to whom and how staffing patterns worked was very important to understanding how decisions were made at various points of the Watergate story."

Doar was adamant that his lawyers sort out facts but advocate nothing. Memos were expected to be clean, clear and crisp. "If they were speculative, you labeled them 'speculative,' " said Hamilton. Altshuler remembered that they did not "speak the language of partisanship. We'd talk about 'the President' instead of Nixon."

Ensconced in the seedy old Congressional Hotel

on Capitol Hill, Doar's lawyers were assigned to bed-
rooms that had been converted into two-desk offices.
"We were supposedly nonpartisan. It was clear as we
got to know each other better that some of us were
Democrats and some Republicans. My recollection is
that John cagily made sure you had a Democrat and a
Republican in the same room," said Hamilton, whose
officemate was Weld, a Republican.

Fraternization with the press was forbidden. Everybody had a story to tell about letters from reporters
eager for pipelines into Doar's operation. Flattery was
another ruse. "How does it feel to be the Jill Wine
Volner of the impeachment committee?" Sam Donaldson, ABC Television's Capitol Hill corrrespondent,
asked Hillary at a press conference with Doar. (Volner
was the leading female lawyer in the special prosecutor's office.)

Once or twice, Taylor Branch, writing for *Harper's*
then, got together with Hillary but he always found it
"a little disappointing" because she would not tell him
anything. Once, Hamilton told Doar that she and her
husband had been invited to dinner by an old newspaper friend. "He looked at me and said, 'Dagmar, I'm
a bachelor, so restricting my social life may be easier
than it is for you, but I'm not accepting any dinner
engagements for the duration.' The message was pretty
clear: cancel the dinner."

There were no social amenities. They relied on
one another for companionship, staying together for
lunch or dinner but cautious of what they talked about
in neighborhood restaurants. "You had to be very careful of anything you said, even to your spouse," Kirk-

patrick said. "I lived in a little apartment hotel with a switchboard. Anytime my husband called and might ask a question, I'd have to decline to answer. We never knew who was listening." Everybody was so immersed in work that the standing joke was that when Easter came they could all pray together at their own sunrise service through the bay window of one of their offices. "The only way any of us knew it was weekends was because people would change from ties to jeans," Kirkpatrick said.

Certainly clothes were the last thing Hillary ever thought about. "She didn't care a flip about them," said Kirkpatrick. Others cared. Since members of Congress dropped in unexpectedly from time to time, there would be subtle reminders to be "professional" in desk, demeanor and dress. Hillary caught on quickly, showing up in a new suit one day that she had bought for an interview in Fayetteville. Though going shopping was something Hillary had never liked, she adapted. "She'd been impatient at first but once she got started, she had a great time," said Kirkpatrick. "Anytime she did anything she was interested in, she went to the nth degree. Shopping was another manifestation of that."

Hillary talked often about the history being made. She and others were sobered by the realization that it was a pivotal time in the country and they were living through significant moments that could bring down a president through a procedure that tested the heart of the democratic system and could very well damage it. "There were lots of ambivalent feelings," Kirkpatrick remembered. "It was a victory in the sense you won a case but there was also a lot of sadness."

126 * HILLARY RODHAM CLINTON

Unlike the rest of Washington, which for two years relied on rumor and the press for clues to the most compelling whodunit in memory, these forty-four lawyers and their support staff were, indeed, the insiders. They had access to information no one else had. They took pride in the extraordinary thoroughness Doar demanded in developing an impeachment case that could be provable several times over. They knew that of equal importance to Doar was the record they built in the House if the case did go to trial in the Senate.

One of the key parts of the case was the tapes that had been secretly made by Nixon of White House conversations. It was expected that somewhere among those hundreds of tapes would be the most damning bits of evidence. The best acoustics expert Doar could find, with equipment far superior to any used by the Senate Watergate Committee the previous summer or by the White House, worked in one of the specially outfitted offices. Several staff members, whose hearing had tested above average, did most of the listening but occasionally others might drop in. Among them was Hillary. What she called "the tape of all tapes," made a lasting impression on her.

"It was Nixon taping himself listening to the tapes, making up his defenses to what he heard on the tapes," Hillary told *The Arkansas Gazette* in 1990. "So you would hear Nixon talk and then you'd hear very faintly the sound of a taped prior conversation with Nixon, Haldeman, and Ehrlichman. . . . And you'd hear him say, 'What I meant when I said that was. . . .' It was surreal, unbelievable."

At least once, Bill Clinton went to Washington

and Hillary introduced him around to her co-workers. The rest of the time they were in constant touch by telephone. While most people in the country were now following the Watergate story, Clinton was paying closer attention than most. He had declared for Congress when none of his friends wanted to challenge incumbent John Paul Hammerschmidt, betting that the fall of Nixon could pull down other Republicans in Congress. Hammerschmidt, the first Republican elected to Congress since Arkansas joined the union in 1836, could be just such a victim.

There was not much doubt among Hillary's colleagues that she was in love and when they finally met Bill, that he was, too. She blushed easily when anyone asked too seriously what plans they had. She confided in one or two friends about the personal battle she waged: whether to marry Bill Clinton and move to Arkansas or try to talk him out of living there. "Taylor," she would implore Taylor Branch through her oversized granny glasses, "have you ever *been* to Little Rock?"

The first time she went to Arkansas the year before, Bill Clinton spent nine hours showing off the beauty spots between Little Rock and Hot Springs, normally a one-hour drive. "Like many people who grew up in Chicago, [I] wasn't even sure where it was," she said in a speech many years later. "I did know that they grew the biggest watermelons in the world." With Terry Kirkpatrick, she talked about the legal profession in Arkansas, how women were treated and whether they were accepted. "I told her it was like everywhere else. Tough. Very tough," Kirkpatrick said. "But I also told her that people generally were fair. You just had to prove yourself three hundred percent. As opposed to one hundred percent."

Were Bill Clinton to win his congressional race, Hillary's dilemma about going to Arkansas would be solved because he would come to Washington. Of course then she would have a second dilemma, that of the congressional wife. In those days few held jobs of any kind and even fewer were trailblazing young lawyers in the public policy or corporate world.

A real measure of Hillary's importance within the Doar inner circle came sometime that spring when she went off to visit Bill in Arkansas. Laughing about it later, she described the deference accorded her—not for her work on the impeachment inquiry staff but because she was the candidate's "girlfriend." But it was nothing like the deference she was shown by John Doar when, upon some new development in the case—memories are unclear as to the precise event, but it had to do with the subpoena of more Nixon tapes—he summoned Hillary back to Washington. Immediately. He would arrange special transportation, he told her—even send a plane.

By late June, Doar's staff had pulled together all the evidence from which the thirty-eight members of the House Judiciary Committee would decide on whether to recommend to the full House that they proceed with impeachment. Rules of secrecy had been so stringent that only Doar and his inner circle, Hillary among them, saw the total effort. Only when everything was proofread in two all-night all-staff sessions and assembled into one comprehensive record totaling thirty-six large black government-type binders did the cumulative effect of what they as a group had accomplished sink in.

"It was staggering," said Hamilton, like others convinced that there couldn't be any other recourse for the committee but to vote to impeach. Yet to come was the incriminating "smoking gun" tape of June 23, 1972, when Nixon approved a coverup of the money trail to his reelection committee.

In late July, the House Judiciary Committee passed by unanimous votes three articles of impeachment. A few days later, the White House released transcripts of the June 23 tape. Terry Kirkpatrick remembered reading it at one o'clock in the morning, standing outside Hillary's office. Now the question in everyone's mind was not so much whether Nixon would be convicted in a Senate trial as whether he would resign.

Then, suddenly, it was all over. On August 9, Nixon announced his resignation.

Dagmar Hamilton remembered feeling "relieved" but with "mixed feelings. If the accusation had gone to trial in the Senate, that would have been a great lesson in civics for the American people as a whole. Without the trial and all the debate and evidence presented there, most people would never really understand the depth of the charges against Nixon, and what it did to the presidency."

Hillary, in a speech to Yale alumni in 1992, called Nixon's resignation "a great relief" and "a great credit to the president, but also a resounding victory for the system that I had studied and learned about here at this school." And in a broader sense, she said that day as the end of Bill's quest for the presidency drew near: "We have a system that truly does work, if only we become involved in it."

The country had held together. Hillary had been part of a high-powered team that had played its role precisely and the right outcome occurred. The procedures and principles that she had studied abstractly in law school and concretely in the cramped offices on Capitol Hill did what they were supposed to. The pragmatic activism that she had felt intuitively was the path to follow in the tensest days of the late 1960s now seemed provably the right choice.

But the end of Nixon was in many ways the beginning of an era for those like Hillary who had been so closely tied to the politics of the times.

"I had to make a decision," Hillary said at Chautauqua, New York, in 1991. "What was I to do? I could have gone to work for a big law firm in a place like Chicago or New York. I could have gone back to work for the Children's Defense Fund, stayed on that career path that for whatever series of motivations I had been moving toward all my life.

"I also knew," she told her Chautauqua audience, "that I had to deal with a whole other side of life— the emotional side, where we live and where we grow and when all is said and done, where the most important parts of life take place."

# 6

# *A Verdict of Love*

*"My friends and family thought I had lost my mind.
I was a little bit concerned about that as well."*

THERE NEVER WAS any "grand scheme," as Hillary once explained it, behind how their lives came together. They made decisions as they went along and marriage was one of them. Almost apologetically, a year after they graduated from Yale, Bill Clinton finally asked her to marry him. "I know this is a really hard choice because I'm committed to living in Arkansas," he told her. "Yeah," said Hillary, who had wanted nothing to do with Arkansas, "it's a really hard choice."

The choice had nagged at them. They talked about it to friends. Bill even talked about it to strangers. One such stranger was Diane Blair, a professor of political science at the University of Arkansas who met him when he stopped to see her in the summer of 1972. He was tracking McGovern delegates to the Democratic National Convention and she was vice chairman of the Arkansas delegation. What impressed her about him was how much he knew about politics. "And though he'd been away at college, out of the state," she said, "he had obviously kept a very close eye on what was going on politically in Arkansas. I remember thinking that here was a young man with a serious political future."

Their conversation was so vigorous and nonstop that she was taken aback when he interrupted her in midsentence to say, "You are making me so lonely for the woman I love." For Blair, suddenly cast in the role of older sister, it was "like a cry from the heart." Words spilled out one over the other as he described an "amazing" young woman named Hillary Rodham. Struck by the intensity of his emotion and curious about why he sounded so disconsolate, Blair asked why he didn't marry this Hillary Rodham. That only unleashed more despair. "My political life will be in Arkansas," he said, "and this is a woman whose future is limitless. She could be anything she decides to be. I feel so guilty about bringing her here because then it would be my state, my political life and my future."

Blair was stunned. She was an ardent feminist, known for her work on the Governor's Commission on the Status of Women and her support of the Equal Rights Amendment—she would debate ultraconservative Phyllis Schlafly on that issue before the state legislature the following year. But she had seldom come across any man who felt as she did or seemed "so sensitive to a woman's career plans and future options. It just won my heart," she said.

It would be another two years before Diane Blair and Hillary Rodham met and then, appropriately, the setting would be political—at the Clinton-for-Congress campaign headquarters in Fayetteville. In the intervening two years Hillary would be struggling to make sense of who she was. By August 1974, the question she faced was even more fundamental: how to begin what truly was the rest of her life?

Suddenly, thanks to Richard Nixon's resignation, Hillary was out of a job but apprehensive about accepting one offered her at the University of Arkansas Law School. Bill was there teaching admiralty and constitutional law when he was not stumping the countryside in his race to unseat the four-term Republican congressman, John Paul Hammerschmidt. She had met a few of Bill's law school faculty colleagues, all but one of them male, on an earlier visit to Arkansas but she had no idea how welcome she would be.

Impeachment staff colleague Fred Altshuler remembered a particularly "poignant" dinner shortly before they all went off in different directions. "I had been in a legal services program in California and I was going to San Francisco to maintain a public interest character to my practice. Friends with me that night were also going into exciting jobs. Hillary, though, seemed to be heading into a professional future somewhat less glamorous than we thought ours were. Here she was, socially committed—and going to Fayetteville."

Hillary had reached the conclusion that she did

not want to stay on the East Coast or go to work for a big law firm. At least not right away. "Much as I would have liked to have denied it," she told the Chautauqua, New York, audience years later, "there was something very special about Bill and there was something very important between us." She decided to take a closer look at Fayetteville and called Wylie Davis, dean of the law school. Was the teaching job he once offered her still open? He assured her it was and that classes started at the end of the month.

"My friends and family thought I had lost my mind," Hillary admitted. "I was a little bit concerned about that as well." Dorothy Rodham, who had wondered if Arkansas would be all that satisfying, told *The Washington Post*: "But you know, I've never told my children what to do. I had to rely on Hillary's judgment—there'd never been any reason not to."

Collecting her belongings, which consisted of a ten-speed bike, some clothes and several boxes of books, Hillary packed Sara Ehrmann's car and together they headed southwest from Washington through Virginia and beyond. Ehrmann remembered their journey into Hillary's unknown future as a "lollygagging, long and aimless trip of stopping and shopping across the South," with Hillary her impatient and captive passenger.

"She wanted to get going but I forced her to do a little sightseeing along the way," Ehrmann said. "We stopped at Charlottesville and I made her look at the University of Virginia. We drove up to Monticello and looked around there. We stopped in Abingdon to see the Barter Theatre where I used to take my kids. And every twenty minutes I told her what I thought about her burying herself in Fayetteville. 'You are crazy. You are out of your mind,' I said. 'You're going to this rural remote place—and you'll wind up married to some country lawyer.' "

When Ehrmann really questioned Hillary's judgment was when they finally reached Fayetteville. "There was this rally going on for the University of Arkansas football team. Everybody in town was wearing those pig hats and screaming *Sou-eee, sou-eee, pig, pig, pig.* I was just appalled." The next day she and Hillary reported for work at Bill's campaign headquarters where scraps of paper and three-by-five cards littered a table, dumped there by Bill. Ever the organizer, Hillary proceeded to bring order out of chaos. Later, hearing Bill speak at a campaign rally, Ehrmann, a seasoned veteran of Capitol Hill oratory, had a change of heart. "I knew then he was going to be president of the United States," she said, "and I didn't question her judgment anymore."

Hillary had no idea what courses Davis would assign her to teach and did not know until two days before classes began that they would be criminal law and criminal procedure. "There was a certain amount of awe attached to Hillary's arrival," said David Matthews, a student of Bill's and a campaign volunteer that year. "Here was this person who had been in on the inner workings of a constitutional crisis that had faced our country. There was a lot of celebrity and notoriety associated with her. Law students, as a general rule, are a pretty cynical lot but there was never a question about Hillary."

Woody Bassett, another of Hillary's students, remembered how she strode into a classroom that first day, "a confident, aggressive, take-charge woman" who employed the Socratic method of teaching. Bill Clinton's style was "more conversational," Hillary's that of "a closer. She came straight at you and after all viewpoints were discussed she used her lawyerly, analytical mind to form an opinion and then offer a concrete answer," said Bassett. "She never left you hanging."

Curiously, if also characteristically, she never discussed her work on John Doar's staff nor any aspects of the impeachment inquiry in her class on criminal law. On September 8, ten days after classes started, President Gerald Ford pardoned Richard Nixon for any federal crimes he might have committed as president. Others who had worked with Hillary on the proceedings said later they had experienced a sense of "outrage" and "betrayal." Hillary kept her views to herself, or at least kept them from her students. "She talked about criminal law," said Bassett. "She was very focused."

She was a hard-driving teacher with a no-nonsense approach to classes. David Gearhart, also a student of Bill's, remembered that "she expected a lot from us and gave a lot in return." The scuttlebutt around the law school always was that Hillary was the better law professor. Certainly, she was the tougher. Bill gave Gearhart Bs and an A, Hillary a C-plus. He admits: "Frankly, I was glad to get it."

In faculty meetings Hillary was equally imposing, insisting that she and her colleagues address university policies affecting women and minorities. She pressed for the hiring of more competent women in faculty and staff positions and, if a report about racial discrimination would come to her attention, would keep after her superiors to get to the bottom of it. She could not bear to have a meeting end before its allotted two-hour time limit and urged her colleagues to fill the unexpended minutes with constructive discussions. She was eager to learn all she could about Arkansas public policy, and when she realized one of the professors was a close adviser to then-Governor David Pryor, she pressed him to discuss with the faculty public policy issues related to the state.

Diane Blair concluded that Hillary "loved teaching" and was exhilarated by her new life. "To be young and in love and intelligent and living in an academic community is a wonderful thing," said Blair. "And when you are interested in your subject matter and able to convey the mysteries of the law, the challenge of the law, to students who are just beginning to understand how complex the subject is, this is enormously gratifying."

Nonetheless, some of Hillary's new friends worried about how this "lady lawyer" with an elite Eastern education would adjust to a small, quiet Ozarks town where Ferguson's Cafeteria was one of the in places to eat; where it wasn't unusual to drive fifty miles to hear Dolly Parton sing; and the season's hostess-with-the-mostest was the one whose Halloween party guests could reach only by way of the cemetery.

As one of two women law professors that first year, Hillary, with Elizabeth Osenbaugh, banded with other women on the university faculty to form a tiny if determined special interest group. At one point, Osenbaugh was asked to write a paper for a Title Seven committee that would dispel one of the stereotyped if basic misconceptions about the proposed Equal Rights Amendment. Recalled Osenbaugh: "It was about why ERA would not require shared bathrooms."

The education of Hillary Rodham on the subject of Arkansas politics, at least, began on similarly fundamental footings. Diane Blair, with the practiced eye of an Easterner who had made the same kind of transition a few years earlier, had learned that there was no percentage in getting angry with the comments and the attitude of people in Fayetteville since much of what was going on was not necessarily mean-spirited or done with malice. "It was just that things hadn't quite come along yet," she said. "What Hillary adapted to was that there were times to be forceful and outspoken and demanding and direct. And then there were times to be patient and persuasive and bring people along with you. She was very articulate but never strident. Strident didn't win. Persuasiveness did."

Among her law school duties was to supervise two programs that were very much in keeping with her vision of what the law was all about: one providing legal assistance to convicted criminals serving sentences in two regional prisons, the other overseeing the school's legal aid clinic in which third-year law students, certified by the dean, handled uncontested cases in court under her supervision. She had been admitted to the bar in 1973, having passed the bar exam on her first trip to Arkansas that August.

Not all members of the local legal community were convinced of the clinic's merit. Those were the days, according to Van Gearhart, David's brother and the clinic's student coordinator at the time, when popular opinion was that "if a person had ten dollars, a car and clothes on his back, he could afford to pay an attorney." The idea that everybody was entitled to legal defense was still controversial. "Constitutional," said Diane Blair, "but controversial."

Gearhart said that Hillary "spent a lot of time placating the bar association and making sure they understood we weren't trying to take cases away from them." In drafting indigency guidelines, she devised an attorney referral system that rewarded those willing to assist her students in supervisory capacities.

"She reassured the local bar and judges by agreeing to accept criminal appointments from the Circuit and Municipal Courts," Gearhart wrote in a 1992 collection of law school reminiscences. "She rightly believed that if we expected cooperation from the local bar, the clinic must reciprocate." At the end of the first year, it was obvious that her efforts had paid off. The clinic had served more than three hundred clients, half of them represented in local courts by her students.

Inadequate legal services was always a concern to Hillary, who did not differentiate between victims and the accused when it came to their right to legal advice or counsel. Gearhart said she was more involved in administration than in trying actual cases, though she handled a few. Women lawyers were rare in Washington County. Hillary sparked interest because she was a tenacious litigator with a sharp tongue, not easily intimidated by the bench. When she appeared in court, good ol' boys from around the countryside who relished an entertaining show came to watch what Hillary called "the talking dog syndrome." They marveled at who she was as much as what she did, just as they might want to watch a "miracle dog," Karen Ball of the Associated Press reported.

In a case involving rape, Hillary appeared before a judge who was the epitome of a Southern gentleman, known for his courtly manners and sense of duty to protect the fairer sex from the seamier side of life. Contending that he would be asking questions "too unladylike" for "Miss Hillary" to hear, the trial judge attempted to exclude her from negotiations. "Hillary had to very adamantly insist to the judge that this was her client," said Blair. "It was the South, remember, and you wouldn't let a woman listen to some of those details."

It may have been Hillary's first criminal case. "I have a vivid memory of Hillary working nights on one felony case," said Van Gearhart. "Due to her aggressive advocacy, she was able to work out an acceptable plea agreement for her client and gain respect for the program."

Rape was an odious crime but few in the community cared enough to do anything about it. "I don't suppose there was any more rape then than later," said Ann Henry, a lawyer and another in Hillary's growing circle of independent-minded women around Fayetteville. "But the women's movement had brought out the idea of women as 'property'—belonging to someone but not having independent thought and action.

Dorothy Howell at eighteen, Class of 1937 at Alhambra [California] High School. An early role model, Hillary's mother belonged to the Scholarship Society, Spanish Club, Girls Athletic Association and Senior Dance Committee. She was also Hillary's best friend, head cheerleader and the sister she never had. She encouraged Hillary to aim high and envisioned her daughter someday sitting on the U.S. Supreme Court. (© *Nancy Kaye 1993, from 1937 Alhambram Yearbook*)

Hugh Rodham, at twenty-three, when he graduated from Pennsylvania State University with a B.S. degree in education in 1935. He was a lifelong Republican who switched only once, when he went into the voting booth to pull the lever for his Democrat son-in-law. Until shortly before his death in 1993, he lobbied President Clinton for a cut in the capital gains tax. Son of an English coal miner who worked in the mines during the Great Depression, he believed in education "for the sake of earning" and as a school-of-hard-knocks tutor lectured Hillary that life was "tough out there." (*LaVie, The Pennsylvania State College, 1935*)

A teacher's pet throughout her school years, Hillary (*lower right*) with her sixth grade class in 1959 at Park Ridge's Eugene Field Elementary School. Elisabeth King, with her hand on Hillary's shoulder, enjoyed teaching Hillary so much that she transferred to Ralph Waldo Emerson Junior High in order to have her in her classroom another two years. *(Courtesy Ernest Ricketts)*

"Goldwater Girl" Hillary Rodham (*left*) prepares to pitch Lyndon Johnson's "Great Society" policies, and self-acclaimed "bleeding heart liberal" Democrat Ellen Press Murdoch (*right*) to argue Barry Goldwater's conservative views in a mock debate at Maine South High School on the eve of the 1964 presidential election. Ready to hold coats is fellow student Matt Bunyan. *(Southwords Student Newspaper)*

Wearing white gloves and a bow in her hair, Hillary (*left*) and Ellen Press Murdoch model their prom dresses while waiting for their 1964 Junior Prom dates to arrive. Hillary was never boy crazy, though she liked boys—preferably older, more mature ones in college. (*Courtesy Ellen Press Murdoch*)

A bespectacled Hillary discards the feminine coiffeurs of her high school days for the more popular stringy look of the late 1960s. A budding activist demanding "change" even as a Wellesley College junior, she found her niche as a campus mediator and consensus-seeker. In February 1968, vying with classmates Nonna Noto (*left*) and Francille Rusan (*right*), she ran for president of the student government. The student newspaper editorialized that none was exactly spellbinding. To her surprise, Hillary won. (*Courtesy of Wellesley College Archives*)

All smiles at the start of the May 1969 Wellesley commencement were (*left to right*) Trustees Chairman John Quarles, Hillary, Wellesley President Ruth Adams, and commencement speaker Massachusetts Senator Edward Brooke. Hillary, the first student commencement speaker in Wellesley's history, turned extemporaneous to take Brooke to task for what she later claimed was a "pro forma" speech that defended Richard Nixon and ignored the issues of the times, including the war in Vietnam. (*Courtesy of Wellesley College Archives*)

Hillary, a first year law student at Yale, wears a black armband in memory of four Kent State students killed and eleven others wounded by the Ohio National Guard during a May 4, 1970, campus protest against the war in Vietnam. Here, as featured student speaker, she and Lucy Benton Benson, president of the League of Women Voters of the United States (*left*), inspect the League's fiftieth anniversary cake. (*Courtesy League of Women Voters of the United States*)

Hillary Diane Rodham, in the Victorian-style wedding dress she bought off the rack the night before the ceremony, and William Jefferson Clinton on their wedding day, October 11, 1975, in Fayetteville, Arkansas. Both were teaching law at the University of Arkansas Law School and getting ready to launch Bill's candidacy for Arkansas attorney general. (© *Ed Lallo*/TIME)

Hillary with Brenda Blagg (*left*), a reporter for the Springdale [Arkansas] *Daily News*, and Brynda Pappas (*right*), a volunteer who had worked with Hillary in Indiana on Jimmy Carter's campaign for president. They reunite at a May 1978 Benton County Democratic rally where Hillary Rodham's husband, Attorney General Bill Clinton, campaigns for governor and Brynda Pappas's boss, U.S. representative Jim Guy Tucker of Arkansas (later to become governor of Arkansas in 1992), runs for U.S. senator. (*Douglas Howard Photo, courtesy of Brynda Pappas*)

Bill Clinton's mother, Virginia Cassidy Clinton Dwire (later Kelley), *left,* his half-brother Roger Clinton and Hillary join the Governor-elect of Arkansas on election night in November 1978 for his victory speech. He would be the nation's youngest governor. Hillary, wearing one of her favorite dresses, had joined the prestigious Rose Law Firm of Little Rock and was rising fast on the national scene as a litigator, advocate of children's rights and chairman of the controversial Legal Services Corporation. *(Gary Speed Photo)*

Chelsea Victoria Clinton was a week old when her parents, Arkansas Governor Bill Clinton and Hillary Rodham, introduced her to the world in March 1980. Like millions of other children, Chelsea would grow up the child of a working mother. In March 1993, a week after entering Sidwell Friends School in Washington, Chelsea showed a rash on her wrist to the nurse, who wanted to call her mother. "My mom's too busy, call my dad," said Chelsea, dialing her dad in the Oval Office. *(AP/Wide World Photos)*

Arkansas' First Family, Governor and Mrs. William Jefferson Clinton with their four-year-old daughter Chelsea Victoria, in the Governor's Mansion at Little Rock in 1984. (© *Jerry Staley/Sygma*)

It was a long-standing historical tradition in the law that women were property and they had been expected to accept it. It was like the assumption that anybody wearing hot pants or miniskirts deserved to be raped."

Then one afternoon, Hillary and a group of angered women gathered at the Henry home to discuss the issue. By the time they parted, they had outlined plans for a community center that would, in time, become the forerunner of a clinic to help rape victims in the area.

What may have surprised Hillary about Fayetteville was how quickly like-minded people could be galvanized into action. "If you care about improving your community and making life better for people who haven't had your advantages, Arkansas is a place you can make that happen," said Diane Blair. "You don't have to pay your dues at endless levels of bureaucracy— in the same way that Bill could immediately run for Congress and then go right for the attorney generalship. If you saw an unmet need in your own community, whether it was an emergency medical program, a literacy program or dental help for kids, if you had a good idea and could persuade a few other people that it was a good idea, you could just go for it."

Social life in academic Fayetteville was not unlike social life in New Haven. Increasingly comfortable with her surroundings, Hillary settled in among interesting people. She and Bill were a popular couple. With friends, they went to movies a lot, talked a lot, read a lot, played a lot—volleyball was very big on weekends and charades hard to escape if Hillary and Bill hosted the dinner. "Try acting out *Being and Noth-*

*ingness,"* said Blair about the title of an existentialist book by Sartre.

Meanwhile, Bill's campaign was in full swing, with help from Hillary's family. Hugh and Tony Rodham thought Bill Clinton's accent was "a tad strange," but nonetheless volunteered as his "official sign putter-uppers," nailing them "on anything that didn't move, and some that did," Tony told *People*. Back and forth from Chicago were their parents. Hillary recalled that despite his lifelong Republican views—"Great arguments, great arguments"—her father answered telephones at Bill's campaign headquarters. President Clinton bore witness to those arguments in a wry eulogy he delivered at a memorial for his "tough and gruff" father-in-law in Scranton, Pennsylvania, in April 1993. "Lord, how they loved to argue," he said of the Rodham household. "Each one tried to rewrite history to put the proper spin on it. It was a wonderful preparation for politics," even though his and Hugh Rodham's common ground was never politics. It was Rodham's daughter, Clinton said.

Hillary and her brother Hugh, back from two years in the Peace Corps and enrolled by then at the university, shared a rented house that fall. This being Fayetteville, not New Haven, Bill rented his own place.

It was the good life on a small scale. "There were wonderful pluses in all this, a tremendous amount of warmth, friendship and caring all around," said Blair. "Far from being an ultrasophisticated young woman who, like the sensitive soul in Sinclair Lewis's *Main Street*, is beaten to death by provincial clods in a small town, Hillary realized you could live your life and be your own person in this very attentive environment."

"People were warm and welcoming to me. I felt very much at home. And it was a shock," said Hillary, "because I had never lived in the South or a small place before. It gave me a perspective on life and helped me understand what it was like for most people."

If Fayetteville neighbors were also curious—the way they tend to be in small towns—48.2 percent of them in the Third Congressional District were politically supportive. They put their votes where their noses were. Hammerschmidt won reelection that November in the only close challenge he had ever encountered, but Bill Clinton, just twenty-eight and in his first venture before an electorate, carried thirteen out of the district's twenty-one counties. They would become the bedrock of his Arkansas constituency. Clinton had been right about Watergate and the backlash, but not right enough to overcome a popular incumbent. And while it may have been what was to be a rare defeat for Clinton, for a political unknown it was a remarkable showing. If he had ever had any doubts, he knew now that he was on the right track.

More cognizant than ever now that marrying Bill would mean marrying Arkansas and his life there, Hillary continued to question whether this was the right thing for them. While she enjoyed teaching, it was no secret that in an academic community change came slowly. Her interests lay in helping set policy. Yale had taught her that policy was made in different ways, including the use of lawsuits and changes in the law. If the system was wrong in certain areas, then you had to find a case that allowed it to be challenged and use that as a vehicle to make change. Hers was among the most activist visions of the legal system.

For a time, at least, Hillary wrestled with career options within the framework of law or politics or a combination of both that would be open to her as a political wife. From a growing network of active married women who befriended her, she began to see that it was possible to keep one's individual identity intact. "She never doubted you could do it. She saw us active with our children and taking part in things we thought important," said Ann Henry, who was chairman of the Washington County Democratic Central Committee when Bill Clinton arrived in Fayetteville. "We felt we could make a life. We were trying to be positive. Hillary, I guess, was watching the kind of life we had."

Bill's dilemma about Hillary became Ann Henry's and Diane Blair's and that of other friends who recognized that she could easily have a political career of her own. "That's what we were agonizing over because we wanted more women to be part of that system," said Henry, who had put her own career in law and teaching momentarily on hold while her children were small. Even so, said Diane Blair, "I never heard her say, 'If I marry him I can't go back to Illinois and run for the U.S. Senate.'"

What Blair did remember was "this endless dialogue we had supporting the women's movement. We spent a lot of time encouraging our women students, who had grown up in Arkansas with a limited sense of what their options were, begging them to see that the whole world was there and they should reach for their greatest potential. Discussions like that made everyone conscious of her own life. So I'm sure Hillary was aware that in marrying Bill she was shutting another door."

After a year in Fayetteville, Hillary decided it was time to get away. She went to Park Ridge and the East Coast. But after interminable conversations with those closest to her, she came back convinced she had not missed anything by moving to Arkansas. People who suspected otherwise, who saw her consumed with unfulfilled ambition, did not know her at all, she said later.

"That's one of the stereotypes that any woman who strikes out on her own has to live with, who has her own career," she told Marian Burros. "I think it's a little hard to reconcile with a lot of the decisions I've made in my life—for me anyway. My relationships and my commitment to those relationships has always, in my mind, been the most important part of my life."

Still, Diane Blair remembered that "right up to the time she married" Bill Clinton, Hillary was "questioning whether she was doing the right thing for both of them."

And what finally tipped the balance?

"Love," said Blair.

Not at all certain of that, Bill Clinton added a nudge of his own when she arrived back in Arkansas and he met her at the airport to drive her to town. Did she remember that house she liked, he asked her—which, of course, she did not. To refresh her memory he pulled into the driveway of a little brick cottage set off by a small stone wall where every spring daffodils planted by some earlier occupant brightened that part of California Drive. They had driven past it earlier in the year, and while she was away he bought it, furnishing it with an antique bed covered by flowered sheets from Wal-Mart. So she would have to marry him, he told her.

"Suddenly, it was just decided," said Blair. Dorothy Rodham arrived from Park Ridge a few days before the wedding to help freshen up with paint some of the walls in Bill's little house and to carry out wedding day arrangements decided upon by her daughter. The night before the nuptials, she asked to see the bridal gown. There was none. Hillary, accustomed to baggy pants and frumpy sweaters, had never gotten around to it. Together, they went shopping, buying off a department store rack a Jessica McClintock Victorian-styled cream-colored dress with high neck, long sleeves and touches of lace.

Then on Saturday, October 11, 1975, fifteen days before her twenty-eighth birthday, with their immediate families and a few outsiders in attendance, including Park Ridge playmate Betsy Ebeling, the Reverend Victor Nixon, a Methodist minister, pronounced William Jefferson Clinton and Hillary Diane Rodham husband and wife.

Over at Ann and State Senator Morris Henry's gracious and sprawling home, a crowd of nearly two hundred friends from all phases of Bill's and Hillary's lives—Park Ridge, Wellesley, Georgetown, Oxford, Yale, Washington, Hot Springs, Texas, Hope, Little Rock—awaited them. Dusk became night as people drifted in and out of the house refilling their glasses from a bubbly fountain of champagne that never ran dry. They talked about the cake—tiered and topped with pale yellow roses—and the newlyweds—"and, of course, politics," as one guest said. But, too, "they were tickled to death over the marriage," said Ann Henry.

There was no honeymoon. Sometime later, Dorothy Rodham came up with the idea of going to Mexico. "We got a special rate, and we all went down together," Hillary's brother Hugh told *People*. A good time was had by all, according to Tony. "Acapulco for ten days." Mr. and Mrs. Rodham, Hugh, Tony and of course, Hillary and Bill.

Throughout that year, Bill had been gearing up to run for Arkansas attorney general in 1976. With an emerging name in the national political arena, his 1974 Congressional campaign had been singled out by the Washington-based National Committee for an Effective Congress as "the most impressive grassroots effort in the country today." Hillary had turned her sights on Little Rock and what she saw was not encouraging.

Confronting her, at last, was the very issue she and her friends had long debated. Was she going to be a traditional political wife and only that? Or was she going to be a person in her own right? "We talked about that among ourselves," Ann Henry remembered. "Part of it comes from the want of a challenge. Do you not do anything? Do you give up your personhood and your own sense of what you are and have to develop? Do you sacrifice that for your husband's ambitions?"

Hillary's answers to those questions would come soon enough. In the news that fall was Barbara Pryor, wife of Governor David Pryor, asserting her own independence as a political wife. When she appeared in public one day with a European kinky-look hairdo, Arkansans let out a collective gasp. From then on it was apparent that criticism about the wife of their governor went beyond a seemingly radical hairstyle.

Aware of the vitriol, Hillary was quietly incensed. Indifferent about her own appearance, which some saw as "frumpy," and others, more kindly disposed, simply dismissed as "unadorned," Hillary belonged to the armband-and-placard-waving rather than the bra-burning school of feminism. Protest, in her book, called for a cerebral approach through writings and speeches.

But here was Barbara Pryor, under attack for preferences and associations that had nothing to do with how her husband ran the state. (The Pryors would, in fact, announce their separation that November.) Here was exactly what Hillary could expect to encounter the higher Bill climbed on the political ladder. "People were hardly aware of wives of most elected officials because they were not perceived to have that much influence," said Henry. "But the minute you hit the governorship, then they see it as a partnership and expect the wife to be perfect."

Myrna Martin, whose husband, Festus, had been Bill Clinton's official campaign manager against Hammerschmidt, remembered a group of friends were out to dinner one night waiting for Bill and Hillary to join them. The moment they arrived it was apparent that there was something different about Hillary. Her hair was frizzed.

"When somebody commented about it, she said it was in support of Barbara Pryor because she thought it was wrong that people criticized her. I thought that was neat of Hillary," said Martin, "I thought that was a real principled thing for Hillary to do."

# 7

# Trials and
# Errors

*"I don't think people paid much attention to me.
But when he became governor, then I had to start
thinking about this role that I had inherited."*

WHEN IT CAME to Arkansas, Jimmy Carter, like
George McGovern four years earlier, got a twofer when
he ran for president in 1976. General elections did not
count for much in Arkansas of the 1970s. If you made
it through the Democratic primary in May, you almost
certainly were a shoo-in come November. Bill Clinton's
easy win over two Democratic opponents and the absence of any Republican candidate wrapped up his
attorney general race early that year. For a big-picture
politician like Clinton, it did not take much to turn
his attention to coordinating a presidential campaign
in his home state for a fellow candidate from the Deep
South, particularly one who had dispatched aides Jody
Powell and Frank Moore to help in his 1974 congres-

sional campaign. Nor did it take much for Hillary, one of the new street-smart politicos destined for bigger things and equally savvy about the long-range potential, to turn her talents to Carter's campaign in Indiana even though, she told me later, she wasn't sure he could win. The first time Hillary met Carter was in 1975 when he spoke at the University of Arkansas. She and Bill had spent more time with him than any of the other Democratic hopefuls of 1976.

Certainly Hillary was primed for whatever lay ahead in Indiana, even if it meant leading a separate life for a while. Married less than a year, she had no children to worry about. She had no career moves to juggle. And while it was true that her husband was running for public office, since he already had it in the bag she had no role to play as The Candidate's Wife. This was a chapter in the ongoing saga of American political wifedom that Hillary would be spared—at least for a few more years. What she learned in the interim would ultimately offset any momentary deficiencies she might have had in the basic arts of receiving-line hand-pumping, tea party trivia or approximating Southern gentility—even if her failure to grasp the larger equation that factored Women, Wives, Family Values and Public Office into a strange 1980s calculus would repeatedly leave her struggling for an answer.

Hillary's agenda in those days was not simply to master the intricacies of political organization but, more important, to make herself known among the Democratic power brokers as more than just an appendage to an up-and-coming young Arkansas politician. Fellow feminist Betsey Wright, who had recognized

Hillary's potential in McGovern's Texas campaign, had encouraged her to go after a job in Jimmy Carter's campaign organization. "I felt she needed to establish her own worth to the possible new Democratic administration," said Wright. "She was one of the best-organized people in the world, so good at drawing out of people more than they ever thought they had to give."

Tim Kraft, Carter's national field director, remembered being lobbied on Hillary's behalf by what he called a Texas "sorority" of extremely tough, highly capable women Democrats who felt she could benefit from further seasoning if a spot could be found for her. Kraft, with Hamilton Jordan and other Georgians, had put together the campaign organization in the forty days following Carter's primary win in Ohio. He remembered, "It wasn't a question of *if* you were going to put Hillary anyplace. It was a question of *where* you were going to put her."

In the greater scheme of things, Jimmy Carter didn't expect much from the traditionally Republican stronghold of Indiana. "It was a tough state," said Tim Kraft, "but they were all tough. The whole Midwest looked tough. And we weren't giving it away either." As a proving ground for an eager young pol like Hillary Rodham, it was as good as any. So in late August she showed up in Indianapolis to help state coordinator Douglas Coulter as his field coordinator running Carter's campaign against incumbent President Gerald R. Ford.

At Indianapolis campaign headquarters, yet another in the string of dingy, run-down buildings the politically committed invariably worked out of in these here-today-gone-tomorrow operations, the euphoric atmosphere made the surroundings almost bearable. Jubilant over Carter's thirty-point lead over President Ford, campaign staffers nearly believed they could nudge traditionally Republican Hoosiers into the Georgia Democrat's column. "They went after it like they were going to carry the state," said Kraft, a native Indianan who probably knew better but hoped otherwise. Ruth Hargraves, an Arkansan who had worked for Senator J. William Fulbright and was hired by the Carter campaign to keep the checkbook under the new campaign spending laws, said the September surge for Carter "was the high point of the campaign."

Hillary, as number two in the hierarchical structure, had learned her lessons well in the McGovern campaign's sagebrush suicide mission. There were not many bloodless battles in state-level presidential political campaigns. In Indiana, the liberal three-term Democrat Senator Vance Hartke was about to pay the piper in a match with Indianapolis Mayor Richard Lugar. And Democratic challenger Larry Conrad was about to become a footnote in his race against Governor Otis Bowen.

Indiana Democrats had been flabbergasted that Carter had bothered to send a team at all, particularly since he was expected to capture the solid South and needed only to split eight critical swing states, of which Indiana was not one. "It was the first time since Lyndon Johnson that a Democratic presidential candidate made any kind of an effort," said William Geigreich, who knew all about unsuccessful runs by Democrats in Indiana and at the time was working on Conrad's race. But Carter was also aware that a number of Indianans in the southern part of the state had ties to Kentucky and Tennessee, and where there were Southerners, there was hope.

While state coordinator Coulter traveled the state, Hillary, quickly perceived as a first-rate organizer, built a bureaucracy of ninety-two counties run by that many people, and coordinated volunteers in cities and townships within those counties. In the process, she built a personal constituency. "If you asked her a question, she'd give you a straight answer," said Geigreich. "She didn't sugar-coat. You never had to wonder. If I said, 'How are we doing in such and such a county?' she'd say, 'You're a disaster. You need to do this. This is what my people are telling me.' You always had a strong sense from her of where things were and what people were feeling."

There were also a lot of nuts and bolts to tighten in running a campaign like Carter's—dealing with the landlord, the budget, the payroll, the ego-stroking of local people and the arrivals and departures of VIPs like Miss Lillian and others in the Carter clan. "She knew who needed to get the phone call, be in the motorcade, sit on the podium," said Brynda Pappas, a campaign volunteer for Bill in 1974 and University of Arkansas acquaintance whom Hillary had brought on board. Days seldom ended before midnight. By Saturday night, Hillary and Nancy Hartley Gaunt, a Vance Hartke operative staying with a prominent Indianapolis lawyer and his wife, would collapse in exhaustion and hysterics to watch the fledgling *Saturday Night Live* cast parody the silliness of Carter's Peanut Brigade, knowing how close to the mark it hit.

During Hillary's first week on the job, she laid out her suggestions for how the staff should cope with the stress-filled days ahead. They almost certainly would end up screaming at one another, she said, but there was no percentage in pouting. Brynda Pappas remembered that Hillary dealt with people by letting them know "that while they might have problems with some larger situation, she didn't have a problem with them. She never made you feel you were the problem or had screwed up in a situation she thought had to be handled in a certain way."

She did not equivocate. William Schreiber, Democratic Party chairman of Marion County who two months earlier had emerged bloody but intact from "a knock-down, drag-out" fight over the delegate selection process, recalled that she had been particularly blunt with him. "She made it clear soon after she arrived that I was still radioactive," said Schreiber. "She said my high-profile involvement would in some cases be a negative force in the campaign in Indiana. So I kept a low profile, coming in during the day but not hanging around at night when volunteers were there."

But Schreiber remembers something else about his encounter with the young law school professor/legal aid lawyer. It was a trait rare in politics and just about any other field: when she gave him the bad news, "I wasn't offended by what she said. . . . And I don't know how she did that."

In disputes, Hillary took no prisoners. "She could

outargue anybody," said an admiring Ruth Hargraves, "and the last thing you wanted to do, particularly if it was at the end of the day and you were dead tired, was disagree with her. You always knew she was going to win." Hargraves and Hillary had quickly discovered they had more than Jimmy Carter in common. As a junior member on the Senate Foreign Relations Committee staff eight years earlier, Hargraves remembered that the only person lower in rank whom she could "boss around" was a fellow Arkansan attending Georgetown University by the name of Bill Clinton.

There was a vague recollection of Bill Clinton appearing on the scene in Indianapolis a couple of times that fall. Some people were aware that he was running for something but neither Hillary, Bill nor anybody else made much of it. She was all business when she had to be and fun to be around when she could relax. What impressed people was her adaptability. "She never seemed to be uncomfortable," said Schreiber, "whether she was talking to a ward-heeler politician or a union representative."

She pushed for the bold decision when she thought the end justified the means. Short on volunteers for the phone bank, she and Coulter decided to advertise for help and offer the minimum wage. Some of the applicants were senior citizens on fixed incomes. Others were "clients" of a bail bonding firm that had occupied space in the campaign headquarters building but recently had moved around the corner—no doubt the reason a neon sign still flashed "Bail Bondsman" above Carter-Mondale posters stuck on front windows.

In yet an earlier life, the space had housed an

appliance repair shop whose former customers strayed in from time to time. Across the street was a city jail where nothing got past its occupants. It didn't take long for the word to get around that behind those postered windows was a bookie operation. Police made a couple of stabs at raiding the place until they finally decided the hundred-telephone bank was on the up-and-up—merely a harmless Carter life raft adrift in a sea of municipal Republicanism. But out of such underdog antics came sustenance for the ragged, out-manned Democratic staffers. Hillary and Coulter joked that staid Republicans never would have had the "nerve" to set up shop in a former bail bondsman's office or partially staff it with accused wrongdoers.

Hillary believed, most of the time, in the glass-half-full philosophy of life and clung to her optimism. One night over a group dinner, faces were long and spirits plunging fast. It had been one of those every-thing-that-could-go-wrong days. There had been a se-ries of damaging side issues that involved Carter's position on a Constitutional amendment restricting abortion and on his own misstated position on tax reform. Finally, Hillary took the floor to make a pitch that almost had everybody convinced. They were at rock bottom, she conceded, so things couldn't get any worse.

Then, with near-perfect Enter-Stage-Right tim-ing, a paperboy walked into the restaurant to hawk Carter's latest disaster. In a freewheeling interview with *Playboy* magazine about his religious beliefs, Car-ter had admitted that he had "looked on a lot of women with lust." What's more, he said, he had "committed adultery in my heart many times."

Hillary was wrong. Things could get worse. What, in September, had all the makings of a Carter landslide had deteriorated by November to a toe-squinching cliff-hanger.

Her earlier idealism had tempered considerably. She and Nancy Gaunt sometimes talked about their wide-eyed McCarthy and McGovern days, times of un-shakable belief in an agenda of change and liberalism. Carter, with his preaching of hard choices for hard times, was seen by some as an antidote to the party's idealistic binge of the 1960s. "It had become clear the Democrats needed a broader appeal," said Gaunt. "Working for Carter, you were aware that you were part of the much larger puzzle."

But ideology was not what Hillary Rodham was about in the Indiana campaign. She was a political technician still growing and learning who fine-tuned her reading of people, their strengths, their weak-nesses, and how best to use them. "She did not waste much time on negative thinking," said Diane Meyer-Simon, who headed Senator Birch Bayh's Indiana of-fice. Despite Bayh's progressive thinking on issues con-cerning women—he was floor leader when the Equal Rights Amendment came out of his committee—atti-tudes were still troglodytic toward women in top-level political jobs. "When I went to speak for Birch, people would say, 'Oh, they sent the blond again.' So I thought it was a very courageous thing for Carter and Hillary to take on Indiana," said Meyer-Simon.

Only a few of Hillary's campaign staffers had gone home to bed by the time Carter became the first Deep South candidate since the Civil War to win the White House. Hillary stayed in Indianapolis to celebrate Carter's triumph. When she went home to Fayetteville, she was armed with names of new FOHs with whom she would keep in touch through the years.

Meanwhile, in Arkansas the idea that the South had risen again to play a major role in national politics—and that the road to Washington could indeed start at the statehouse as it used to in the old days—made Attorney General–elect Bill Clinton's first victory in elective politics all the sweeter.

About to realize the first formal step in his long-standing ambition to devote his life to public service, Clinton pledged to protect individual rights against "arbitrary government." And he won the hearts of enthusiastic consumer groups ready to lend support when he took on the state's utility and business interests. Behind the scenes, Hillary played a crucial role, advising him on policy, staff and other matters just as she had started doing when they were living together at Yale.

As attorney general, Bill's salary was about $26,000 a year, thanks to a pay raise passed by the legislature taking effect that year. Teaching law carried with it an $18,000-a-year salary but to earn it Hillary would have had to stay on in Fayetteville. Despite whatever youthful aversion she once might have had about "making money for some big anonymous firm," she now wanted to join a big if not necessarily "anonymous" law firm. "I thought maybe I'd start practicing when I got to Little Rock, but there were not any women in any of the major law firms," she told James Merriweather of *The Arkansas Gazette*. "There were not many women lawyers, period." Elaborating further some years later, she said there weren't any role models except "the traditional male model. That model went to lunch with people, that model took people out for drinks, that model played golf," she told Marian Burros. She was not devaluing such business rituals, because they were important in getting people to know one another. "It's just harder," Hillary added, "when you have other responsibilities at home."

Herb Rule, self-described "point person on recruiting" for the then small but prestigious Rose law firm in Little Rock, met Bill Clinton when he ran for Congress in 1974. When he got the word from Bill that Hillary would be hanging out her shingle, "I tracked her down," Rule told *The American Lawyer* in 1992. For Hillary, it would be the start of an ongoing education. Touched with what William R. Wilson, Jr., one of Arkansas's more dynamic and colorful trial lawyers, called "celestial fire," the Ivy League–educated Hillary was a stellar prospect for the firmament of any house in Little Rock's legal community.

Hillary joined Rose as an associate on February 1, 1977, less than a month after Bill became the state's top law enforcement officer. Her new job, not in keeping with traditional activities of political wives in Arkansas, lifted a few eyebrows at the time. Later, critics would be loudly questioning whether she could separate the interests of her clients from those of the state government by then presided over by her husband, the governor. One of the oldest law firms west of the Mississippi River, Rose was well entrenched in state business long before Hillary joined it, but her critics contended that Rose clients enjoyed an unfair advantage in dealing with the state while Governor Clinton's wife was in the firm.

Certainly, the Rose connection provided Hillary the flexibility she needed to pursue her interests in children and disadvantaged families. She helped found Arkansas Advocates for Children and Families, a statewide program providing legal assistance. And through speeches and essays, she addressed the issue of children's rights.

Her 1974 essay, "Children under the Law," for the *Harvard Educational Review*, had earned her some attention and also caused some confusion among academics and legal theorists. In it, she argued both for more state power and more individual responsibility, that because of the disparity between newborns and teenagers, courts should consider on a case-by-case basis whether children are incompetent. In constructing her case, she used slaves, wives and Native Americans as historic examples of classes of people without legal prerogatives to control their own lives.

At Rose, she gained the reputation of a hard-driving lawyer who moved between family law and commercial litigation but also was clearly interested in stretching into public interest and criminal law. Since Rose almost never took the latter, she looked outside her own firm. Wilson said she approached him about representing what he called "accused citizens."

He knew her as a law school professor who had

successfully appealed to the Arkansas Bar Association's House of Delegates for help in funding the university's then-new legal aid clinic. "She was unbelievably talented, well informed, passionate—just about everything that a person trying to persuade somebody ought to be," said Wilson, who joined in the vote to give her what she wanted.

When she came to him three years later, defense lawyer Wilson would have hired her himself, he said, but "it might not have been consistent with being the wife of a political person because criminal practice keeps you pretty well tied to the courtroom." There was also the very real possibility of conflict of interest were a criminal case to go up on appeal. If that happened, the attorney general—her husband—would have had to disqualify her and hire outside counsel. "And that," said Wilson, "would have been a nettlesome problem."

Nothing like that happened in the year and a half that Wilson "associated" her. Their first case was defending a man charged with aggravated assault on his girlfriend. Wilson recalled that Hillary gained a friend for life when she referred to the defendant by his given name rather than the nickname "Tiny" that disparaged his weight. But more important, Wilson had assumed the case would end up in a trial. To Wilson's great surprise, Hillary, showing her meticulous attention to detail, won it on preliminary hearing for lack of probable cause—a neat trick for any criminal lawyer, but particularly for one who had not spent much time in trial work.

What Wilson admired was her "steel trap mind"

and an ability to "read through a batch of documents and get the essence as quickly as anybody I've ever known." Women trial lawyers were still a courtroom oddity who "may have been looked upon as a little unfeminine, but Hillary helped dispel that myth," he said. "She was very definitely feminine." Using the ultimate Arkansas compliment for a spellbinding preacher, Wilson said, "She had a good mouth on her."

Hillary's reputation as a lawyer who specialized in cases involving children was spreading. In El Dorado, Arkansas, she teamed up with Beryl Anthony, a local attorney who would be elected to Congress the next year, to represent the foster parents of a two-and-a-half-year-old boy whose biological parents wanted him back. "Contrary to what the rules say, that you can't fall in love with your ward and you can't seek adoption," Anthony said, "the foster parents came to me and said they had cared for him for two and a half years, felt like he was theirs and didn't want to give him up."

The case was not unlike the one Hillary worked on five years earlier with New Haven Legal Assistance attorney Penn Rhodeen when experts testified that the child would suffer long-range psychological harm if taken from the foster mother's care. That time the judge ordered the child removed. This time the judge ruled in the foster parents' favor when Rodham and Anthony proved that the contract the foster parents had been required to sign with state authorities was null and void and therefore not enforceable.

The case never was appealed. Had it reached the Arkansas Supreme Court, it could have become precedent-setting, of significance not just in Arkansas but in the nation. But the team of Rodham and Anthony drew some consolation from the fact that the case was so dramatic in terms of how ineffectual the state's foster program was that when Hillary became First Lady she used it as an example of how the regulatory system needed to be improved. "We said it was intolerable for a child to be left two and one half years someplace when you call it 'temporary.' That really got Hillary fired up."

During that same time, Hillary also became involved in a legal controversy that both put her personal beliefs to work and put her smack in the path of the conservative revolution that was building steam even as the Democrats were trying to organize a government. In late 1977, Jimmy Carter rewarded Hillary for her efforts in his Indiana campaign by naming her to a two-year term on the three-year-old Legal Services Corporation, a nonprofit, federally funded program that provided legal assistance to the poor, often through community-based legal aid programs.

The LSC was a concept Hillary firmly endorsed. For years the idea had been pushed hard by many liberals—including people such as the legendary Chicago community organizer Saul Alinsky—who believed that expensive legal services had long been unfairly denied to poor people in cases ranging from landlord-tenant disputes to the right to government-financed medical benefits. One controversial case involved an LSC affiliate suing the government for the sex-change operation of a patient who couldn't afford it. The conservatives believed it was insanity for the government to pay to sue itself. They also feared that free lawyers would provoke a flood of politically motivated lawsuits. The right, resurgent in the late 1970s and casting about for issues, launched an assault on the LSC that was as loud and unrelenting as anything they did, making it a totem of the Reagan Revolution and eventually gutting the program after some bruising battles in Congress. In the middle the whole time was Hillary Rodham as chairman. As with so much of both Hillary's and Bill's careers, the job was a prime opportunity to build relationships that would later prove essential: among those sitting on the board with her was Mickey Kantor, the Democratic activist lawyer and fund-raiser who would later chair the Clinton-for-President campaign and become the U.S. trade representative.

Meanwhile, Hillary continued to use her maiden name both professionally and privately. "It was not a fierce, feminist statement, but a practical concern," said Diane Blair. "That's what I wanted to do," Hillary told *The Arkansas Times*, but also, "it seemed like a sensible way of keeping my professional life separate from [Bill's] political life. I sensed that this was territory I needed to walk through pretty carefully. I did not want to be perceived as a conduit to him." Not that the name wasn't an issue almost from the first moment. No sooner had Bill announced his candidacy in 1976 than a reporter asked him if he thought Hillary's use of her maiden name might hurt him politically. "I hope not," he replied.

By 1978, when Bill first ran for governor, whatever she called herself professionally, Hillary was still supposed to be The Candidate's Wife. "I think I failed to appreciate how important in political terms an elected person's spouse is to the voters," Hillary told Mara Leverett of *The Arkansas Times* years later. "In retrospect, what I didn't appreciate was how personally people viewed those things. When Bill was attorney general, that's not such a high-level position, and I don't think people paid much attention to me. But when he became governor, then I had to start thinking about this role that I had inherited. That's when I had to come to terms with it on a personal and emotional level."

Not that it made much difference that year. Nineteen seventy-eight was Bill's year and he was on a roll. The young native son had quickly asserted himself as a fresh and popular force in Arkansas politics, barely warming the AG's chair before making a run at the Governor's Mansion. There were a lot of reasons to yell at this endlessly confident Ivy Leaguer with the down-home drawl—his wife's name was low on the list—but there were also a lot of reasons to like him. For those who cared, he was promising to pull Arkansas into the last half of the twentieth century. And almost before folks knew what had happened, he'd won—sweeping through the Democratic primary and swamping a hapless Republican to become, at age thirty-two, one of the youngest governors in the country's history.

And that made Hillary Clinton not The Candidate's Wife but The First Lady. A year after her thirtieth birthday, she was going to have to come to terms with a new set of circumstances that might have been challenging for someone with another decade's maturity. Even she was unprepared for the demands made upon her as the state's First Lady while at the same time pulling her weight among her Rose colleagues. There were some pluses, however. No matter how little business she brought into the firm, her bosses would not fire her. And, to some extent, the public was already conditioned to governors' wives who asserted their independence.

Barbara Pryor, by taking what she later would call her "year off from marriage" to Governor David Pryor in 1975 to seek her own identity, returned to college, went into the movie-making business and eventually helped her husband win reelection. "It is possible to keep your identity and be married to a politician, to have a separate career," she told *Good Housekeeping* magazine in 1977. "I believe the voters will understand and respect you for it."

A few years earlier, Jeannette Rockefeller, wife of Republican Winthrop Rockefeller, had asserted her independence though not out of an uncertain identity. While not a "professional" in the sense that Hillary had a profession, but with all the money she wanted, Jeannette Rockefeller did what she pleased. Absorbed in public policy and by social issues that interested her, she accepted speaking engagements if the forums suited her purpose. Unconcerned by political fallout since strong political headwinds indicated that Winthrop would never go further than governor, she frequently failed to make appearances at official functions they gave if they were irrelevant to her own agenda.

Hillary, on the other hand, managed to maintain a balance between an active public schedule and involvement in issues she cared about. She continued to write on the rights of children. In a refinement of her 1974 essay, she contributed to a collection of papers by Columbia University's Teachers College. Like the earlier one, this work, published in 1979, would provide fodder for her husband's political opponents a decade later when critics accused her of being more of an activist for the "feminist elite of working mothers" than for the interests of their children.

The Rose firm promoted her to partner in 1979, its first woman to be so anointed. While she "took domestic matters on," Vincent Foster, Jr., a key litigator with whom Hillary worked (later to be deputy general counsel in the White House), told *The American Lawyer*, "it was not something that we were trying to encourage or promote at the law firm. So while she continued to do some family law quietly, she really was trying to build her commercial litigation practice."

Around the firm, she was known as a regular-guy type who could put her feet up on the desk and talk as readily about baseball or politics as she could about law. She was supportive of new lawyers, giving them chances to show their stuff. Jerry C. Jones, who joined Rose in 1980 and worked with her in the litigation and labor section, remembered how she responded late one Thursday when a case came in involving unfair competition and trade secrets. "We worked almost around the clock for the next three days, gathering all the facts, preparing affidavits, putting the complaint together and getting it filed," he said. "What amazed me was that she was doing a couple of other things at the same time. She'd leave for a couple of hours and

I'd find out later that she had an engagement at the mansion because she'd bring back cookies." More gratifying than the cookies, though, was Hillary's attitude. "She never treated me like an associate," Jones said. "She'd treat me as a professional."

In the summer of 1979, Hillary and Bill went to England, visiting Oxford and his haunts as a Rhodes Scholar but also taking in the sights around London. "We were trying to have a child, something we were working on," Hillary told Eleanor Clift for *Newsweek* in 1992. "And it was this glorious morning. We were going to brunch and we were walking through Chelsea, you know, the flowerpots were out and everything. And Bill started singing 'It's a Chelsea morning.' Remember that old song? Judy Collins's song?" (The one Joni Mitchell wrote and first recorded.) The significance of that later became apparent when a daughter was born to them on February 27, 1980—by coincidence, the birthday of William Jefferson Blythe, the father Bill Clinton never knew. They named their baby Chelsea Victoria, as much a sentimental salute to that romantic pause in their ambition-driven lives as to their favorite song at the time.

Chelsea had come two weeks earlier than expected and when Hillary arrived at Little Rock's Baptist Medical Center, because of the baby's position in the womb, doctors decided to perform a cesarean section. Talking about it to Marian Burros twelve years later, Hillary described Bill as adamant about being present. He and Hillary had prepared for the birth by taking a course in the Lamaze method of childbirth. He had to be there, he argued.

"We had a little discussion about it," Hillary said. "He was the governor but they were worried that as a father he would pass out or fall flat and cause more of a commotion than a help. Eventually, they were convinced that he wouldn't."

Everything was "wonderful"—for a few days. The three of them roomed together at the hospital, with Chelsea back and forth between her parents and the nursery. "I think for a long time, because his father died before he was born, Bill didn't believe he'd ever live to be a parent," Hillary said. "That was something almost beyond his imagination."

But it was an election year in which the issues would be reduced in time to their simplest common denominators—the Five Cs, as in Cubans, Car tags, Coattails, Carter and Clinton. The Sixth C, as in Chelsea, would emerge as a simple birth announcement. "I think that really disturbed people," Hillary told *The Arkansas Times*. "It set up a kind of dissonance between me and other people and kept them from hearing anything else I might have to say."

The way Hillary remembered Arkansas newspapers reporting Chelsea's arrival:

GOVERNOR BILL CLINTON AND HILLARY RODHAM
HAD A DAUGHTER.

# 8

# Mistaken Identity

*"I kept my maiden name. You would have thought that I had decided to do some terrible deed equivalent to killing the firstborn."*

THE FIRST THING the First Lady of Arkansas and the first woman partner in the 160-year history of the Rose law firm did after Chelsea Victoria Clinton was born was take four months off from work. "I had advantages that other women didn't have," admitted Hillary Rodham.

And, indeed, she did. In the rarefied world of powerful elected officials where the perks included rent-free mansions staffed by full-time cooks, housekeepers, gardeners and security guards, Hillary was doubly blessed by belonging to a prestigious law firm that valued her association so much that she was encouraged to arrange her schedule to suit her personal needs. She fully acknowledged that compared to most women with families and jobs she was atypical. And fortunate.

Yet, even for Hillary, life had its tradeoffs. It had been no accident that she was regarded in the Arkansas legal community as a scrappy, straightforward, very smart litigator. She had worked hard to earn that reputation. And a decade later the Rose firm's managing partner, William Kennedy III, teasingly suggested that her full potential was yet to be realized. She would have been a "superb lawyer," he told *The American Lawyer*, if she had concentrated on her practice and given up living two lives. A former CEO at Rose seconded that motion. "I was always mad at her for not doing more [legal] work," twitted C. Joseph Giroir, Jr.

Actually, in the three years since joining the firm in 1977, Hillary had led three lives. In addition to practicing law and presiding over social and ceremonial functions at the Governor's Mansion, she had added a string of other accomplishments to her curriculum vitae: founder of Arkansas Advocates for Children and Families, chairman of the Governor's Rural Health Advisory Committee, chairman of the Legal Services Corporation and board member of the Children's Defense Fund, the latter two based in Washington, D.C.

They were only a few of her activities as an increasingly visible advocate of children and the disadvantaged, all of which took an enormous amount of her time. But Hillary was committed to public service and often quoted John Wesley, the founder of her Methodist faith, who exhorted his followers to "do all the good you can, by all the means you can, in all the ways you can, in all the places you can, and all the times you can, to all the people you can, as long as ever you can."

Now, added to all of the above, was yet a fourth life. "You can't substitute time, when it comes to motherhood," she said of those early months nurturing her infant daughter. After five years of marriage and wanting children ("It just didn't work out for us," she told Roxanne Roberts for *Redbook* in 1993), and twice that many years concerned about them from a theoretical and legal standpoint, Hillary was learning the practical side of child care.

Her pregnancy had not been easy, according to friends who believed her heavy schedule may have contributed to Chelsea's arrival two weeks earlier than expected. Overjoyed that she had produced her "one perfect child," as she once described her offspring, Hillary was like any other first-time mother pushing the panic buttons of parenthood. While still in the hospital and breast-feeding Chelsea, she thought she was killing her when milk started running out the baby's nose. "Well," the nurse told her, as Roberts recounted the incident, "if you hold her up a little higher that won't happen." Another of Hillary's favorite stories about Chelsea had the infant crying nonstop despite being rocked nonstop. "Chelsea," Hillary said, "we're in this together. You've never been a baby before and I've never been a mother before. We're going to help each other understand all this."

In July, Hillary extended her leave by dividing two additional months between part-time at the office and part-time with her daughter. By September, she had eased back into a full-time schedule with the Rose firm by setting her own hours and, when necessary, having work sent home to her. Being able to spend time with her baby, she later told Marian Burros, was one of the reasons she became "such a big believer in parental leave."

By now, Bill Clinton was in the midst of his campaign for a second term. So was Jimmy Carter, self-incarcerated in the White House Rose Garden by his crippling obsession with the Iran hostage crisis. Arrayed against him was Ronald Reagan at the head of a churning conservative revival. What would come to be called the Reagan Revolution was in full cry with right-wing Republicans taking charge and targeting liberals from the U.S. Capitol to the state houses.

Arkansans already were peeved at Bill Clinton's friend Carter for dumping thousands of Cuban refugees at Fort Chaffee. The Cubans, who had fled Cuba in the Mariel boatlift, were equally unhappy and in late May several hundred broke out of their confinement, charged to the outskirts of nearby Fort Smith and nearly provoked a bloody confrontation with residents. The first warning sign that incumbent Bill Clinton might be in for trouble came the next day when Arkansas Democrats cast their protest votes in the primary election. Capturing 31 percent of the vote by opposing a Clinton-backed increase in car tag fees was a seventy-seven-year-old turkey farmer who made running for office an avocation.

Republicans seized upon the results as a flicker of voters' estrangement. Once wounded in the primary, Clinton suddenly was seen as vulnerable in a number of areas in his gubernatorial reelection bid. His opponents raised doubts about factors that Diane Blair, in her book *Arkansas Politics and Government*, said "could not have turned the tide had not the angry atmosphere, originally created by the car tag increases, already existed in rural counties." Most insidious among those factors was what Blair called "the 'unmanliness' of the governor, reflected in his wife's retaining her maiden name."

None of that was apparent at the time to Clinton, his aides or Hillary, according to Rudy Moore, Jr., who, as chief of staff, was one of the governor's curly-haired, bearded young "triumvirate" of advisers that first term. One reason, Moore wrote in *The Clintons of Arkansas*, a collection of remembrances published in 1993 by the University of Arkansas, was that neither Bill nor Hillary seemed to be "fully engaged in the campaign of 1980."

According to Moore, Hillary had always been "crucial" in her husband's previous races but for this 1980 reelection bid neither one had the focus. "She ordinarily was a perfect balance to Bill, who tended to trust everybody and sometimes to be hopelessly optimistic," Moore wrote. "She saw the dark side of events, and she could see that certain programs and ideas wouldn't work. She would say, 'Bill, don't be such a Pollyanna. Some of these people you think are your friends aren't.' "

The question of who was a friend and who was not had troubled Hillary since Bill became governor. She lamented to a Fayetteville friend that it was "hard to know who your friends were" at that level because "everybody wanted to be the governor's friend."

Moore was among those who thought Hillary's role was always more that of a top-level aide than a policymaker—albeit one with the most secure of relationships. Though the unfathomable part of a political partnership such as the Clintons' was that only they can describe with certainty the influence of one upon the other, Moore said he doubted she ever tried to substitute her judgment for Bill's. "He was always seeing the positive side of things and Hillary had a good propensity to see the negative. She was very good at reminding him of that." In dealing with others, particularly someone she thought was an enemy of her husband's, she would not hesitate to make her opinions known. "If she didn't have any use for somebody," said Moore, "she would tell Bill, 'tell the staff.' And that's what I liked about her."

The "chief criticism" about Bill, according to Moore, was that "he told people what they wanted to hear and then didn't follow through on his commitments. . . . He simply wanted to help every person he could, and he hated to disappoint anybody if he thought there was any merit at all in what they wanted." Taking a side and making the call was "against Bill's nature," Moore wrote in *The Clintons of Arkansas*. "And that is where Hillary often provided some balance."

Among Clinton's aides, there had never been any question about Hillary's importance in his political life. Moore said her political instincts were "at least equal to Bill's though their approaches might differ." In disputes with the staff, Hillary usually prevailed. "At a political level," laconically wrote Stephen A.

Smith, another in the governor's "triumvirate," in his recollection for the University of Arkansas publication, "I also found myself disagreeing with Hillary on two occasions, once on a matter of overall campaign strategy and once on a particular tactical choice. I developed a strong admiration for her persuasive abilities and, thereafter, found someone else with whom to disagree."

Whatever the Clintons' distraction in 1980—fatigue, an absorption with Chelsea, overconfidence or something else—it continued throughout the campaign, according to Rudy Moore, who, because he was on the state payroll, was not supposed to be involved in the campaign. "Hillary had her baby, the law practice and a lot of things going on," he said in an interview. "And Bill's political insincts took a temporary vacation. I literally begged him to make some changes in the campaign. I brought it up all the time. People would tell me what was not happening, but I couldn't get him to reach those decisions."

Even under normal circumstances, without the added pressures of a campaign, political life could turn family life upside down. But clearly, something was more than normally amiss. One theory, whispered about but never proved, was that the symptom or the disease was marital problems. Certainly the Little Rock rumor machine was as well oiled as any in a seat of power and the one in Arkansas had been churning out unsubstantiated reports about Bill Clinton's private life ever since his first run for governor. It was, for instance, around this time that a former Little Rock television reporter and lounge singer named Gennifer Flowers would later claim her twelve-year affair began with Bill Clinton. Those friends and aides who knew Clinton at the time say they saw no evidence of extracurricular activities on the governor's part. Yet, in his traumatic 1992 interview with *60 Minutes*, Clinton acknowledged "causing pain in my marriage."

Though he never spelled it out and never quite said he had had affairs as rumored, his words seemed an implicit admission. "You know," Clinton told *60 Minutes* interviewer Steve Kroft, "I can remember a time when a divorced person couldn't run for president. And that time, thank goodness, has passed. Nobody's prejudiced against anybody because they're divorced. Are we going to take the reverse position now, that if people have problems in their marriage and there are things in their past which they don't want to discuss, which are painful to them, that they can't run?"

The timing and the extent may never be known. But whatever the reality, the Little Rock rumor mill was at least equal to it. And it was a particular vulnerability in a Bible Belt state in 1980.

Attractive, gregarious and charismatic, Clinton was an easy target for gossip. "If you were a member of the far right, obsessed with sexuality issues and repressed like all these Baptist preachers are about all that, wouldn't you talk like that?" said Joan Campbell, a Little Rock friend of both Clintons. "It's hard for other people to take the religious right seriously, but believe me, this is what we've lived with here forever. It's what backs the Ku Klux Klan, what backs the segregationists and Orval Faubuses. This is Southern politics."

Little Rock was no different from anyplace else when it came to political groupies. Women generally "on the prowl" were easily identifiable. "Whether you're male or female, people in power positions seem to attract certain kinds of people," said Rudy Moore. "I thought Hillary was so confident in their relationship that she dealt with that stuff pretty well." Not unaware of the potential for temptation or misinterpretation, Moore said he made it a practice to screen all of the governor's visitors and nothing got past him. Women stopped by from time to time—Gennifer Flowers was never among them, he said—and "I either saw to it that they didn't come in, or if they did, that somebody was in the office with him."

But Clinton may have been his own worst enemy in such matters. Moore once fired a campaign aide who had taken the governor to a nightclub. Clinton liked being with his friends, said Moore, and if they happened to be at a nightclub, well, that was the way it was. Innocent entertainment or not, Moore saw the bigger problem and did what he could to head it off. "I had warned this guy to quit letting him go to those places," he said. "They came back this particular time and sure enough, they had been to a nightclub. I told him, 'You pack it up. That's it. You're not driving anymore.' I was trying to get the point across that you can't take a gubernatorial candidate to a nightclub."

Betsey Wright, Moore's successor from 1983 until 1990, told David Maraniss of *The Washington Post* that "ninety-nine percent" of the stories about Bill Clinton were not true. "And there is one percent where I didn't know where he was. I think there was a lot of wishful thinking on the part of some women. Things that were not." She acknowledged to Gail Sheehy for *Vanity Fair* "the frustrations I went through in the seven years of being his chief of staff, of watching the groupie girls hanging around and the fawning all over him. But I always laughed at them on the inside, because I knew no dumb bimbo was ever going to be able to provide to him all of the dimensions that Hillary does."

But contributing far more to Bill Clinton's vulnerability that election year than gossip about his rumored extracurricular activities had been the so-called rural rebellion. Arkansans, who relied heavily on motor vehicles, were furious about the governor's support of hefty new licensing fees. They were also angry at Jimmy Carter for unloading thousands of Cuban refugees on the state. With a friend like that, who needed enemies?

Moore said he and others around Clinton only realized how much trouble Bill was in a few weeks before the election. "But even on election day we all thought he would pull it out though maybe not by much. It was a big shock when he did not. One of the greatest mistakes we made was that when we realized the gap was closing, we didn't tell people, 'Don't throw away your vote.' "

Whatever their mind-set, thirty-one thousand more voters cast ballots for challenger Frank White, a Little Rock savings and loan executive who had deserted the Democratic Party in order to run against Clinton as a Republican. Riding the crest of religious fundamentalism that year, White saw his triumph as "a victory for the Lord." He would gain inglorious fame soon after he took office by signing—without reading—the state's Creation Science Act. It required Arkansas public schools to devote equal time teaching both the theory of evolution and the idea of creationism, the literal word-for-word interpretation of the Bible's description of how the world and mankind got their starts.

White became the first Republican in nearly three decades to force an incumbent Democrat out of office. Like everybody else—including many who later said they voted for him "to teach Clinton a lesson" but had not expected him to win—White was stunned. None more so than Clinton, however, who later attributed his loss to a combination of the current issues and the public perception of him as insensitive and arrogant. "I simply didn't communicate to the people that I genuinely cared about them. I think maybe I gave the appearance of trying to do too many things and not involving the people as I should."

In a moving farewell address to the Arkansas legislature, Clinton, with Hillary and ten-month-old Chelsea at his side, asked Arkansans to "remember me as one who reached for all he could for Arkansas." Hillary had been angry at first but then turned philosophical, the way she told her high school friend she would deal with defeat, and resigned herself to the outcome. Said Betsey Wright, persuaded by the Clintons to move to Little Rock in preparation—even then—for Campaign 1982: "Hillary has a very enviable ability to separate her personal feelings from the task at hand. She was not going through all the self-flagellation that Bill was."

Wright told Gail Sheehy for *Vanity Fair* that Bill "got crazy in the incessant quest for understanding what he did wrong, which was masochistic." Rudy Moore disputed "postmortem" accounts that Bill was "devastated" and "lost in the wilderness" as he analyzed reasons he lost. Clinton himself called it a period in which "I would seize everything," as Sheehy recounted it. Hillary's explanation to Sheehy was that he "viewed his father's death [before his own birth] as so irrational—so out of the blue—that it really did set a tone for his own sense of mortality. . . . Not just in his political career. It was reading everything he could read, talking to everybody he could talk to, staying up all night, because life was passing him by."

So now, the once-promising young leader had become the vulnerable, vanquished, penitent supplicant whose future seemed uncertain. "There was some concern that since he'd lost half the time when he was running [his 1974 congressional race and now this], perhaps this would be his last chance, that his star would not rise brightly again," said Jerry C. Jones, a Clinton friend.

J. Wayne Cranford, a Little Rock advertising executive who had known Bill Clinton as a high school youth working in a reelection campaign of Senator Fulbright, said both Clintons became better people as a result of his defeat. "From then on, Bill committed himself to deserving to be reelected. And perhaps for the first time, Hillary, who had stayed behind the scenes but was always very much a part of the strategy, was really committed to helping him."

In the election aftermath, Bill, a Baptist and by his own definition "an uneven churchgoer for a long time," was joined at the mansion by three Pentecostal ministers, holding hands with him and praying together as they reassured him that even if he had lost they loved him. About that time, Bill and Hillary joined a group pilgrimage to Israel led by the Reverend Worley Oscar Vaught of the Little Rock Immanuel Baptist Church, who would become Bill's spiritual mentor as the decade went on.

Back again in Little Rock, Bill grappled with his future and what to do with it. He briefly considered becoming chairman of the Democratic National Committee, then decided against it. "I remember that he asked me what he should do," said Jerry Jones, Hillary's colleague but also an FOB from the 1974 congressional campaign. "I said, 'Get a job and go to work.'" He did, joining his friend Bruce Lindsey's law firm of Wright, Lindsey & Jennings. The association provided him the opportunity to make another pilgrimage, this one throughout Arkansas sounding out people about where he had gone wrong.

"I knew at some deep-down emotional level that I would have to run again in 1982 in order to live with myself the rest of my life," he told writer Roy Reed, a University of Arkansas journalism professor, who described Clinton's unofficial survey results in his recollections for *The Clintons of Arkansas.* "They told him he had become uppity, people resented his Ivy League style and his staff had been unresponsive."

Hillary's career, meanwhile, was moving ahead. When she started out at the Rose firm, she had taken on domestic matters and made a name for herself in child custody cases. Now, with encouragement from her partners, she was trying to build her commercial litigation practice. One of her early successes was a breach-of-contract case involving the $3 million purchase of Little Rock's KLRA radio station. "She was still a *young* lawyer at the time," Alston Jennings, Sr., name partner in the losing law firm where her husband practiced briefly between campaigns, told *The American Lawyer*, "but she was not particularly *green*."

The contrast with Bill's aborted political career was striking. She listened as he evaluated his mistakes and was deeply troubled by one in particular: the issue of her name. "I kept my maiden name. You would have thought that I had decided to do some terrible deed equivalent to killing the firstborn," she told the Chautauqua, New York, audience in 1991.

Betsey Wright knew that "the issue of Hillary's name was not a dominant theme. No more so than the young bearded aides, no more so than the working wife and making more money than he did. It was part of a pattern of symbolism—just that Arkansans thought the Clintons were different and better than they were. Hillary had always said she never wanted to hurt anybody and that she had kept her name for her own professional reasons after they got married."

Friends, some serious and some amused, listened as Hillary talked about the issue. "I think she told me she was thinking about doing it [changing her name] and I said, 'Look, what's important is how you feel about it. How anybody else feels about it is irrelevant,' " said Susan Thomases, a lawyer and strong feminist ally of Hillary's. Diane Blair remembered a "teasing conversation" when her husband, attorney James Blair, would tell Hillary and Bill: "If this is a problem, let's do it right. Have a ceremony on the steps of the capitol where Bill puts his booted foot firmly on her throat, yanks her up by the hair and says, 'Woman, you're going to go by my last name and that's that.' Then wave the flag, sing a few hymns and be done with it." Vernon Jordan, the Washington insider and Hillary's friend since her Wellesley days as a member of the League of Women Voters' youth advisory board, recalled that "early one morning she was cooking me and Bill grits and I told her she had to start using her husband's name. She understood."

But it was not until February 27, 1982—Chelsea's second birthday—when Bill Clinton announced that he was running for governor again, that Hillary followed up with a simple statement of her own: she was changing her name. "I was stunned when she did it," said Wright, who was a major planner in Bill's comeback. "I had no idea it was coming at the announcement ceremony. It was a choice only she made. It was not something Bill had asked her to do or that I asked her to do or that showed up in the benchmark poll we took. Believe me, the majority of the people in that state probably didn't care about her name or her law practice, but enough did that it began adding up to a majority if Bill was going to run again."

Hillary made it official on May 3, 1982, a few weeks before the Democratic primary, when she filled out a new voter registration card and signed her name as "Hillary Rodham Clinton." The name wasn't the only change. There was other evidence that she was recasting her image. She had new clothes and a softer new hairstyle and her pretty face had been freed of its spectacled hardware.

Her transformation had the desired effect, even at the office. "I thought, 'Man, she's pretty good-looking all the sudden!' " said fellow litigator Jerry Jones. "I used to kid her about it."

While Arkansans could take some satisfaction in having influenced Hillary's decision, it also was clear that she was a woman unafraid to cut her losses. "I just decided that it was not an issue that was that big to me when it came right down to it," she told *The Washington Post*.

By shedding untraditional trappings like that, Diane Blair said, "this would strengthen Bill's ability to communicate easily with people about how much he was one of them, cared about them. And maybe part of feeling more comfortable with him was their having a sense of Bill and Hillary as a more traditional family unit."

Indeed, her self-transformation served as the ultimate proof of her consistently unemotional and analytical approach to politics; she was able to treat herself as she would any political asset. She had always been that way, but the 1980 defeat seemed to crystallize many lessons that would prove invaluable in the years ahead. One such lesson, a keystone of the 1992 presidential strategy, was never to let a charge go unanswered, and by the end of that 1980 race she knew she was an unanswered charge. "You have to learn how to take political attacks seriously but not personally so that you don't let them interfere with who you are," she told me in 1992. "You deal with them in whatever terms they come to you."

She learned other lessons during Bill's forced two-year "sabbatical" from elective office. Friends who knew a side of her the public did not, said that "as she gained more self-confidence she became more fun to be with, more upbeat, more at ease. She always had good ideas but during those two years that he wasn't governor I think she really became a different person from when she had been adamantly Hillary Rodham," said J. Wayne Cranford, whose friendship went back to her Fayetteville days. "Frankly, I liked Hillary a lot better than I did when I first knew her."

She, too, had been a victim of the Reagan Revolution. Though renominated by Carter for another term on the Legal Services Corporation, Hillary's confirmation was blocked by Republicans in the Senate. Ronald Reagan managed to all but emasculate the program, telling the American Bar Association that he wanted "to explore possible alternatives to the monolithic federal approach to legal problems of the poor."

(The Republicans had long memories and Hillary's stewardship of the controversial LSC would provide political fodder for them in 1992 in the form of campaign directives—referring to her repeatedly as just plain "Hillary" despite deferential titles for others—circulated at the highest levels inside the White House.)

Hillary's career continued in high gear but with

adjustments. No longer the governor's wife, with a built-in support staff, she juggled marriage, motherhood and career much as increasing numbers of other women were doing. While always superbly organized, she accommodated her professional life to her private life. "The most important thing in my life is my family—my daughter and my husband, particularly my daughter because I think you have to put children first," she told Marian Burros in the 1992 interview.

With her priorities clearly established, she organized her work as a lawyer so that there would be time for Chelsea at the beginning and the end of each day and even during the day, while her daughter was young. By the time Chelsea was in the first grade, Hillary and three other mothers taught a supplemental science class twice a week. "That to me was more important than taking time to lunch with my colleagues," she said.

Her own mother had been a strong role model as Hillary and her brothers were growing up. Dorothy Rodham had done "an absolutely superb job," Hillary told the Chautauqua audience in 1991, but had done it as "a full-time mother," there when her children came home at lunch and after school. Hillary's generation had chosen professional careers and there were no easy answers to how their own marital and parenting responsibilities would fit in. "That kind of tension and struggle between the redefinition of adult roles and the needs that children have to have met is one of the defining struggles of the past twenty years," she said. "It is acted out in our homes, in our communities, and it has societal repercussions that we're only beginning now to understand."

In time, Hillary would turn to her parents for help in her own parenting responsibilities. There was always someone to look after Chelsea when Hillary wasn't home, but when the child was seven, Dorothy and Hugh Rodham sold their home in Park Ridge and moved to Little Rock for what some speculated was a step toward Governor Clinton seeking the presidential nomination in 1988. From then on, it would be Dorothy Rodham who cheered Chelsea on at softball games, ballet performances and school functions if Hillary was on the road. The child also may have been strongly influenced by her grandmother's Methodism when Bill and Hillary left the choice to their daughter of whether to become a Southern Baptist, like Bill and his mother, or a Methodist, like Hillary and her parents.

Nor did Hillary take her marriage casually. "I know for a long time the idea of marriage, for me, was not as clear as it certainly was for women of an earlier generation," she said, "because I didn't know how it would fit in with this new personality or person that I was developing." Learning that marriage was a "one hundred to one hundred" percent proposition was difficult. "Keeping in mind what's really important and eternal, as opposed to the mundane problems of every day that are often the things that irritate people and get them upset with each other, is really essential," she told Burros. She and Bill had "matured together, had been through a lot together, helped each other a lot, always loved and respected each other. Yet even with that it's not been easy. It's just something you have to be committed to."

Feminist though she was all her adult life, she would discover during that turning-point period when Bill Clinton came of age as a political figure to be reckoned with that she had far more in common with the "traditional" political wife than she once might have believed. It was a dilemma that would not go away, no matter how accomplished she became in her own right. When the Clintons moved back into the Governor's Mansion in January 1983, her abilities and resources would again be called upon by her husband. But here, too, Hillary's priorities dictated her actions.

"I have a very clear sense about what I think is important to do," she said, "and I try not to be persuaded to do what is important to other people—but not to me."

# 9

# *Making
# Her Mark*

*"It was a risk. People said, 'Well, if she does
something, she'll make people mad. And if she
doesn't do anything, she'll make people mad.'
It was a no-win situation."*

THE PROBLEM WAS as old as Arkansas and they were sitting around talking about it when Bill Clinton concluded that overhauling education could be the most important thing they ever did.

The linchpin would be the chairman, someone who understood what was at stake and was unafraid of the fallout. Expertise in education was not the requisite skill any more than expertise in health care would be ten years later. What counted was political deftness, getting various groups of people to agree on something that would not be totally palatable to any of them. Strategizing and public speaking would be paramount in the hard sell. So whom should he name chairman?

The way Bill later remembered it to writer Roy Reed, Hillary had the answer.

"I think I'd like to be it," Hillary said. "Maybe I'll do it."

Bill Clinton had been right. The single most important thing the two of them ever did for Arkansas was to modernize an antiquated public school system. For all her earlier misgivings about whether it was her kind of place, after Hillary marshaled the support Bill needed in 1983 to put through his education-reform package there was no longer any doubt that she and Arkansas were meant for each other. Virginia Kelley said her son's choice of Hillary to chair the state's new Education Standards Committee was one of the smartest moves he ever made. "It gave Arkansas an opportunity to know her."

It was also a political tactic as calculated and bold as it was potentially hazardous, but for Bill Clinton, who was making his political comeback, it would provide the jumpstart he needed. Virginia Kelley had been more than a little skeptical, not of Hillary's credentials—after all, she knew something about teaching from her two years on the University of Arkansas Law School faculty—but because she was family. "That would be like asking me to do it. I didn't know if this was going to work or not," Virginia said. "I thought, 'Oh, my God, the man has lost his mind!' " Among doubting politicos, it wasn't so much a question of Bill Clinton's sanity as it was how serious he was about reforming education if he was willing to make his wife the chief reformer. Some predicted that Hillary's stewardship would prove fatal to his career.

Arkansans, who savor politics almost as much as fish fries and joked that they used to elect governors every two years just so they could combine the two, took readily to Hillary's particular political style. She described it as the kind with "the small p," and meant "advocacy on behalf of issues and positions and causes" to improve the quality of life for the majority of people. Steering clear of partisan or ideological fights, she believed, as her friend Diane Blair once assured her, if your idea was good and you could persuade a few other people of that, "you could just go for it."

Hillary went for it, the second time in that many years—to her "financial disadvantage," she'd say later—because "I believed in what I was doing." "She's made a lot of sacrifices for me to be in public life," said Bill of the Clinton family's principal breadwinner. "But neither one of us ever cared about getting rich." He didn't know if naming her chairman was a "politically wise move," he said, but he believed it was "the right thing" to do. "This guarantees that I will have a person who is closer to me than anyone else overseeing a project that is more important to me than anything else." Far from a cosmetic whitewash committee, Clinton made clear that this was to be the political equivalent of putting all your roulette chips on red.

For years, Arkansas education had been batted among extremist mentalities—from the segregationist Orval Faubuses to the creationist Frank Whites—and a general sense of disaffection. Attempts to overhaul the nineteenth-century school system usually were stymied by people who considered property taxes not just excessive but unfair. Diane Blair, writing in *Arkansas*

*Politics and Government*, described Arkansas as "trapped at the bottom ranks by a vicious cycle of factors and attitudes, including an attitude that Arkansas schools were as good as they need to be."

Bill Clinton vowed in his inaugural address that year that his number one priority would be putting people back to work. "So many people in Arkansas have seemed to believe as long as I've been alive that in some sort of strange way God meant us to drag up the rear of the nation's economy forever," he said. To effect any long-range economic revival, education had to be the key.

"He needed someone not only to bring people together but to define, clarify the issues, develop solutions and then sell the program," said Skip Rutherford, who once headed the Arkansas Democratic Party and met Hillary when he was on the Little Rock School Board. "By naming Hillary, he sent a signal to the state that not only was education a critical problem and important issue but *the* issue of his administration."

"It was a risk," Hillary told *The New York Times'* Burros. "People said, 'Well, if she does something, she'll make people mad. And if she doesn't do anything, she'll make people mad.' It was a no-win situation. But our perspective was different than that. We thought that if you were committed to trying to make change in public life—it was what I cared about and it was his agenda—then we ought to put ourselves into it and do everything we could to make those changes."

Just how urgent was the need for reform was pointed up that spring by an Arkansas Supreme Court ruling that the state's funding formula for schools was unconstitutional—in effect denying students equal access to educational opportunities by allowing rich districts and poor districts to spend widely divergent amounts of money. To sell the need for change, the Clintons turned to the format they knew best: political campaigning. Bill built support for a tax increase by warming up the people who would pay for it and the people who would vote it into law. And Hillary, with fourteen committee members, went on the stump to each of Arkansas's 371 school districts to solicit feedback from citizens and to explain why new standards were essential to stem a "rising tide of mediocrity," which recent studies showed was becoming a national blight on education.

Hillary was an exemplary surrogate as well as a persuasive spokeswoman. As the beneficiary of a superb education in Park Ridge, Illinois, public schools, she was appalled by the limited curriculum offered Arkansas youth. Hugh and Dorothy Rodham had been unrelenting taskmasters about the value of a good education. "Learn for the sake of learning," Dorothy used to tell her children. "Learn to earn a living," their father would add. In an interview with *Paris Match*, Dorothy said she used to tell her daughter that school would be "a great adventure" where she would learn many things and experience new passions. "I motivated her so that she wasn't simply resigning herself to go to school. I wanted her to be enthusiastic to the idea. It may be for this reason that Hillary was never afraid. Not of school. Not of anything."

For millions of immigrants and first-generation Americans in the early part of the twentieth century, education was the opening scene in the American Dream. Hugh Rodham's football scholarship may have spared him a possible future as a coal miner—or a factory worker, which his English-born father had been from the age of thirteen. Dorothy Rodham's strong feelings about a good education may have come from her mother, who, according to the U.S. Census records of 1920, did not read or write by the time she was seventeen.

Aware of the sacrifices parents made for their children's education, Hillary had little patience with youths who felt shortchanged by Arkansas schools and gave in to a self-pitying inferiority. She told Roy Reed she never forgot one particular student in the criminal law class she taught who couldn't answer a question. "I kept after him and after him, and finally he just threw up his hands and said, 'Why don't you leave me alone? What do you expect? I just went to school in Arkansas.'" She was "furious," she told Reed. "I couldn't understand what had prompted that, and I really was angry. To seek refuge behind this 'poor me, I'm just from Arkansas' mentality was, to me, unacceptable."

Nor did anybody in Arkansas forget that Bill Clinton was the product of those schools, least of all Bill Clinton. "In my family, starting with my grandparents," he told Reed, "there was every presumption that I could do anything I wanted to do; that I had the same opportunities that anybody else had, if I worked hard enough. And they set out to make sure that I did work hard enough."

The state of education in Arkansas had troubled

Bill and Hillary for a long time. During Bill's first term as governor, they initiated an annual High School Day when honor students from around the state were recognized at the Governor's Mansion. Once-potentially "poor me" students had attained heights their families might not have thought impossible. Overcome with emotion, time and time again parents told the Clintons that their child was the first in the family to graduate from high school. Many could not go on to college because a required basic math or science course was not part of the school's curriculum. Said Betsey Wright: "The impact on Bill and Hillary's commitment to improving education in Arkansas was enormous."

Hillary and her committee traveled the state for four months listening, fostering discussions and synthesizing ideas from parents, students, teachers, administrators and anybody else with a vested interest in a literate citizenry. From the consensus they came to, they drafted proposals and Hillary became their advocate across the state. Put as much emphasis on the quality of academics as you put on athletics, Hillary would urge audiences. What education needed was "discipline, teamwork and standards," she told the Pulaski County PTA. Give teachers "the same support and praise for teaching children to read and write as we do those who teach them to throw a ball through a hoop." The emphasis on athletics being what it was, "That was kind of radical," said Little Rock columnist Ernest Dumas.

What would become "the most misunderstood thing about the education reforms"—teacher competency—first emerged as a committee "finding," not a recommendation for standards, according to Wright. Some Arkansans said they opposed any pay raises for teachers; others said they knew of teachers who should not be teaching at all. "It also showed up in a public opinion poll we did," said Wright. "It was so clear that the quality of teachers was the kind of complaint that Hillary and others on the committee heard throughout their hearings." At a press conference that September, Hillary released the committee's preliminary report. "Quit making excuses" about the cause of the education system's dilemma, she said, and recognize that a school "that passes illiterate and semiliterate students commits educational fraud."

Among the group's key proposals were capping class sizes at between twenty and twenty-five pupils, lengthening the school year from 175 to 180 days by 1989–90, requiring that foreign languages, advanced mathematics, chemistry, physics, art and instrumental music be taught in every high school, toughening up graduation requirements, providing more counselors for elementary and high school pupils, and setting up a state-administered Minimum Placement Test given in the third, sixth and eighth grades, with a mandatory 85 percent pass rate.

Endorsed by both the state Board of Education and the legislative Joint Interim Committee on Education, the proposed standards were taken to the citizenry about a month before Clinton called the legislature into special session. Betsey Wright described a statewide lobbying effort using radio and television advertising, direct mail and phone banks, paid for by $130,000 in private money raised by Clinton staffers and support-ers. "No legislature has ever come as close to being begged to raise taxes as that one was when it finally convened," said Wright.

Incorporated in Bill Clinton's education-reform package, when he sent it to the legislature, was the teacher testing program, which, according to Diane Blair, "may have been the keystone in coalescing public support [but] earned Clinton the passionate enmity" of the Arkansas Education Association (AEA). Many teachers were "enraged that they were being asked to do this demeaning thing of taking a test to see if they were fit to be in the classroom," said Blair. "And a lot of their antagonism was vented in a very tangible way toward Hillary." In an interview years later Hillary said she had been "deeply hurt" by the reaction but had held her ground because she saw "so clearly" that insisting upon teacher competency would "lead to an increase in the status and the respect of a profession I value."

"She stood by her husband on everything, pub-licly," said Wright. "They are each other's harshest critics, but she knew it was the only way we were ever going to get more taxes. Almost everybody had an experience with a teacher who couldn't spell or add or something."

The Clintons' effort appeared doomed, however. The governor's proposals to raise income taxes, corpo-rate taxes and severance taxes on the production of natural gas went down to defeat in both houses when the legislature convened in October. The only one that remained on the table was a one-cent sales tax increase and it was opposed by a coalition of labor, consumer and community organizations because it did not exempt food and utility bills. When the AEA attempted to block passage of a Senate bill, Clinton threatened to kill the tax increase, which would not only eliminate funds to implement the new standards but do away with teachers' raises.

Into the legislative fray went Hillary the Eloquent, her mission of oratory to soften up reluctant lawmakers caught among the forces of the teachers' lobby screaming "witch hunt," small school districts fearful of extinction through consolidation, and the coalition, some of whose holdout members were believed to be softening if they could only be assured of teacher accountability.

"After the First Lady's impassioned speech to old-guard state legislators about demanding more of Arkansas children and teachers, Representative Lloyd George of Danville, a cattle farmer who was Clinton's peskiest critic and a protector of tiny country schools, leaped to his feet," wrote Dumas in *The Minneapolis Star-Tribune* in 1992. " 'Gentlemen,' he exclaimed, 'we've elected the wrong Clinton.' "

Sid Johnson, an AEA member who served on the National Education Association board at the time, said later that "we believed that the Chamber of Commerce, in particular, said, 'Look, we're not going to support a sales tax increase unless you give us accountability of those teachers.' " As for school district consolidation, Wright said, "There was always a tremendous fear on the part of people who represented tiny school districts. They were so scared that all of this was coming basically from disdain for tiny school districts, and Hillary's respect for any school district that would maintain standards was very obvious. It became impossible for them to argue against the littlest schools having the same kind of opportunities for kids as the big schools."

By the end of October AEA resistance had collapsed and the legislature gave Clinton his sales tax, the first such increase in twenty-six years. Wrapping up her committee's report that December, Hillary called the proposed standards "a blueprint that Arkansas can follow over the next few years." The following March, in approving the standards, the state board of education ordered them to take effect in June 1987.

The teachers' debate with the Clintons over testing raged on, however. "We sort of feel like combat veterans," Hillary told a meeting of education reporters in Atlanta in March 1985 while everybody waited for an Arkansas state court to rule on the constitutionality of the tests. A few days later, the court dismissed the teachers' lawsuit and the next day twenty-five thousand teachers took the test. Of the 10 percent who failed, a majority were black. Bill Clinton, on CBS's *Face the Nation*, denied the test was discriminatory. Hillary did not back down either, insisting to *The Washington Post* that no teacher should have failed and that the 10 percent who did "touched thousands and thousands" of young lives.

Sid Johnson, later to become AEA president, told of running into Hillary at a state legislative committee hearing in Little Rock in 1990 and being invited to accompany her a day or two later to two speaking engagements at education events in other parts of the state. Teachers were still very angry with the Clintons, said Johnson, who did not want to be "co-opted" by being seen with Hillary but respected her and was curious about what was on her mind. For three hours, facing each other in a two-passenger plane as they flew across Arkansas, they talked about everything from their childhood to the state of education in Arkansas.

He told her about that morning in 1985 when he woke up to hear a radio announcer saying "Well, well, well, the teachers of Arkansas are having the tables turned today. They're taking a test instead of giving one." It had set the tone for his entire day and had left him thoroughly disgusted with himself, he said, because in looking back, what teachers should have done was to have boycotted the new standards and let the state hire replacements for them all.

He remembered that Hillary just listened as he described taking the test, "whizzing" through it and later, outside the classroom, "feeling so bad that I wanted to kick the building. I told her it was the worst day of my professional career." Her response, though, had told him "worlds" about what she had gone through—the name-calling, the hissing, the hate-filled demonstrations. "It was mine, too," Hillary said.

Even ten years later, old animosities continued to fester. A March 1993 *Wall Street Journal* essay, head-lined "Mrs. Clinton's Czarist Past," attempted to cast doubts on just how effective Hillary had been as a task force leader. To bolster his arguments, Blant Hurt wrote that American College test scores showed little, if any, progress in reading, writing and math skills among Arkansas high school students during a twenty-year period ending 1992; that while Scholastic Aptitute Test scores were at a ten-year high, only 6 percent of Arkansas high school students took the test; that 22 percent of eighth-graders in the Little Rock school district failed the Minimum Performance Test in 1991. "As Arkansas's education czar," noted Hurt, a Little Rock business columnist, "she approached her job as a social engineer who centralizes and bureaucratizes, rather than as a market liberal who respects local autonomy and defers to the wisdom of market forces."

Not all of Hillary's old adversaries remained holdouts. The Clintons are notable as people who may lose battles—or at least not win conclusively—but still turn some opponents into allies. When Clinton ran for president, on Hillary's list of unofficial but sanctioned spokesmen was Sid Johnson. (And people were still asking about Hillary and education because she continued her crusade. In April 1992, she and others on her standards committee, as part of what she called a ten-year "retrospective," met with the board of education to discuss changes they thought should be made.)

The school initiative paid off. A measure of how far both Clintons had come in the ten years since Bill's first political campaign were the honors bestowed on them in 1984. The National Association of Social Workers named them Public Citizens of the Year; *The Arkansas Democrat* named Hillary Woman of the Year; *Esquire* magazine listed them among 272 baby-boomers, culled from five thousand nominees, as the nation's best and brightest, recognized as recipients of "a torch

. . . passing between generations . . . approaching the full bloom of adulthood." Of those chosen on the basis of their "courage, originality, initiative, vision and selfless service," 23 percent were women. Hillary's affiliation with Rose law firm was duly noted but so was her work as head of the Arkansas Education Standards Committee.

But 1984 proved to be significant for more than the accolades. If the 1960s had been politically and socially turbulent and the 1970s trying in terms of career decisions, the 1980s would be fraught with emotional land mines in the Clintons' private lives. Topping the list was Roger Clinton, Bill's half-brother, who was arrested in Arkansas that summer and convicted that fall of drug trafficking.

"It was like every worst nightmare you ever had come true," said Betsey Wright. "People kept talking about how the New Hampshire primary and all the Gennifer Flowers and draft stuff had to be the lowest point in Bill and Hillary's lives. But that was a piece of cake compared to the pain they went through over Roger Clinton's drug arrest and addiction. That's because it was real, it was true, it was personal and it was someone they loved."

Supporting the undercover investigation of Roger by the Arkansas State Police was only part of Governor Bill Clinton's "nightmare." "I couldn't tell my mother, or her husband or my brother," he said. "Bill became very introspective, did a lot of reading about co-dependence," said Wright, his chief of staff at the time. Together, Bill and Hillary undertook an intensive study of drug addiction. Later, in family counseling sessions, Bill looked at how his own childhood experiences had shaped his life.

Born in 1946 to the widowed, twenty-three-year-old Virginia Cassidy Blythe, Bill was four years old when his mother married Roger Clinton. He was a Hope, Arkansas, car dealer but also an alcoholic who physically abused Virginia—"he never did strike me *a lot*," she told me in 1992—and "emotionally" abused his son, Roger, and stepson, Bill, who assumed the dual role of family protector and peacemaker. "One of these days," Virginia Clinton Kelley said she told the senior Roger Clinton, "it won't be Bill who gets even with you. It'll be your own son." Sixteen years after "Big Roger" died of cancer, she saw that grim prediction come true when young Roger's addiction to cocaine was disclosed.

"Bill felt in a lot of ways there was a fine line between what happened to Roger and what happened to him," said Wright. "People say my number one weakness is that I'm conflict averse," Clinton told David Maraniss for *The Washington Post*. "I think part of that is I'm always trying to work things out because that's the role I played for a long time."

In Hillary's lexicon of tribulations, young Roger's "trouble" would be a key point of reference. Nothing in her and Bill Clinton's lives together, "as I know or care about," she said in the aftermath of campaign charges in 1992 when Bill's character became an issue, compared to that 1984 family ordeal. "That was difficult," she said, "that was stressful."

If their detractors saw an arcane quality to Bill and Hillary's relationship that would dog them into the White House, of more immediate interest to their supporters in the 1980s were the Clintons' political ambitions. Hillary shrugged off speculation that she might run for public office. "I like having a role as a private citizen making a public contribution, and I'm really lucky my husband is the kind of man and governor who wants to involve me in his work," she told the Associated Press in 1985. "And I'm pleased that I can help do what he's basically trying to do, and that's provide a better future for the state."

Instead, she focused on her law practice and developed the Rose firm's intellectual property and patent infringement practices; joined corporate boards like Sam Walton's Arkansas-based Wal-Mart, whose Environmental Concerns Committee she chaired at a time when her husband was coming under increasing attack by environmentalists; cut ribbons to open shelters and clinics for neglected and disadvantaged children; chaired the New World Foundation, an organization funding civil rights and other liberal-oriented causes whose board included her old allies Vernon Jordan and Pete Edelman and which had helped Marian Wright Edelman start what later became the Children's Defense Fund.

No single crusade would equal or recapture the drama of her work for education reform, but she was no less committed to improving the health and education of children and youth. In media parlance, she was "good copy." Hillary Rodham Clinton, went the headlines in those years: "Says Her Work for Education Not Finished"; "Discusses Decline in Infant Mortality in Arkansas"; "Lambastes AEA at AFT Conference in Washington"; "Leads Effort for HIPPY Program for Pre-School Children"; "Praised for Role in Bringing Progress to Arkansas."

Few political wives were as secure—or a more visible campaign target. Frank White, the creationist former governor trying to unseat Bill Clinton in 1986, promised that his wife would be "a full-time First Lady." He went after Hillary's law practice, charging her with conflict of interest as a partner in a firm doing business with the state government. "Remember, Frank," taunted Bill, a line that proved effective enough to resurrect and rewrite six years later against George Bush, "you're running for governor, not First Lady."

It was not the last time her law practice would provoke charges of corruption. Presidential hopeful Jerry Brown's accusations along those lines in 1992 provoked more than her quip about staying home and baking cookies. "As far as I know," she said during the uproar, "I'm the only lawyer related to a public official that I'm aware of in this country who had actively practiced law who has never even shared in a penny of state funds that have ever gone to my firm." According to *U.S. News & World Report*, partner Webb Hubbell said that Hillary shared none of the money paid by the state under terms of her partnership agreement. Nor did she share in fees that the firm earned from representing bond underwriters. (By 1988, Hillary made the *National Law Journal*'s list of "100 Most Powerful Lawyers." Countered *The American*

*Lawyer* four years later, she had only tried five cases, one in the last decade, while associated with the Rose law firm.)

While the Clintons were inured to the brutal business of politics by now, Chelsea was not and when she was six, Hillary told interviewers, they started to prepare her for what life might be like as the daughter of a politician. They introduced her to supermarket tabloid journalism and staged mock debates in which one or the other of them played the opponent, saying things like, "This Governor Clinton has done a terrible job." Why would anyone say such a thing about her daddy, Chelsea would ask. "I don't know," replied her father, "but we just want you to know it may happen."

By 1987, Clinton watchers speculated that there was no place left for Bill Clinton to go but Washington. At age forty-one, the kid from Hope faced the very real question: to run or not to run? By late spring, Gary Hart's sexual peccadilloes caught up with him, forcing him out of the race and raising questions that presidential hopefuls could no longer ignore: were the media's old hands-off practices concerning a candidate's infidelities a thing of the political past? Were candidates' private lives finally fair game for public scrutiny?

In a last-minute change of mind that surprised even his mother, Bill Clinton announced he would not be a candidate in 1988. Standing beside him, eyes blurred by tears, was Hillary. He'd like to be president someday, he said, but "my heart says no. Our daughter is seven. She is the most important person in the world to us and our most important responsibility. In order to wage a winning campaign, both Hillary and I would have to leave her for long periods of time. That would not be good for her or for us."

Added Hillary: "I want to go to supper with my husband. I want to go to the movies. I want to go on vacation with my family. I want my husband back."

In Michigan a few days later at a National Governors Association meeting, Hillary's composure had returned when a reporter asked how the Hart decision was affecting discussions among governors' wives. "It's very tough talking about alleged stories," she said. "This is the other thing you learn in this business. People can say anything with total impunity because there ain't nothing you can do about it. You're not going to sue for libel; you just hope it will not have any effect."

Out but not forgotten, the Clintons continued their presidential pursuit. At the University of Virginia in Charlottesville in the summer of 1989, they joined President Bush at his "education summit." As cochair, Clinton was a major participant in drafting a half dozen national education goals to be met by the year 2000. Hillary had her own agenda: child health issues, one of which—infant mortality—found the United States ranked about nineteenth. When she told that to Bush at a luncheon, he didn't believe her. The U.S. health care system was the envy of the world, he insisted. Not so, said Hillary, citing more figures. Unconvinced, Bush said he would get his own statistics. He did and the next day, he gave Bill Clinton a note from an aide confirming that the United States ranked nineteenth, worse than any of the major industrialized nations in the West. Bush had scrawled at the bottom: "Hillary—I was wrong on the figures. You were right!"

Accustomed by now to speaking her mind, Hillary dropped by a photo op the following spring to take on a Democrat who wanted her husband's job. Challenger Tom McRae hadn't expected the First Lady of Arkansas as a stand-in when he called a press conference to accuse Clinton of being too pigeonhearted to debate him on the issues. Yet, sure enough, there stood Hillary demanding to know: "Do you really want an answer, Tom? Do you really want a response from Bill when you know he's in Washington doing work for the state? That sounds a bit like a stunt to me."

Arkansans split not just politically but generationally as they argued over the proper role of a candidate's wife. In a tongue-in-cheek analysis, *Arkansas Gazette* columnist Deborah Mathis offered some "good spouse" rules. Among them: "Find a certain place and stay there. Political trenches are no place for a lady."

For some ladies, perhaps, but this, after all, was Hillary. You could take Hillary out of the political trenches, maybe, but you could never take the political trenches out of Hillary. Earlier that year, speculation ran high that she might go after Bill's job if he decided not to seek reelection. "I believe a lot of people urged her to run. When she went around the state for education reform, she developed a great number of friendships and had a big following of her own," said longtime party stalwart William Jernigan, who became chairman of the Arkansas Democratic Party in 1991.

Hillary finally scotched the rumors. "I just want

to wait and see what happens and make the best of what I'm doing at the time, and that's always worked for me," she told *The Arkansas Gazette*. Any decision she would make about seeking an elective office would come only after her husband's political career ran its course. "If he made the decision not to do it, then I might think about it," she said. "But I really don't have any future plans. In this political business, you can't really plan, anyway."

Maybe not, but you can explore. It was the summer of 1991, the summer of the coup d'état against Mikhail Gorbachev, that Bill and Hillary got three or four intimate friends together one Saturday morning in the kitchen at the Governor's Mansion. The economy was going nowhere. The news from the Soviet Union wasn't comforting. There was definitely a vacuum in Washington that somebody had to fill. The question at hand: should Bill Clinton try to fill it?

Everybody was devil's advocate that day, laying out the what-if scenarios that included Mario Cuomo, New York's Hamlet-on-the-Hudson, and some other possibilities like Missouri Congressman Richard Gephardt and Tennessee Senator Albert Gore. "We thought we could put some money together," said Craig Smith, an aide to Governor Clinton. "You had to have enough money to get the message out and it was everybody's feeling that the message would resonate. But it was always a crap shoot. You get ten people in the race, one who comes out and then you have to go up against an incumbent president. We were throwing the long ball."

Finally, Bill, Hillary and Bruce Lindsey just

looked at one another. "So what happens if we win?" Lindsey asked of the very long-shot possibility that Clinton might actually wind up with the Democratic nomination. "Let's just get there first," said Bill. Hillary had another answer.

"We'll change things," she said.

# 10

## *They Shoot Candidates' Wives, Don't They?*

*"You always get angry when people lie about you, but it doesn't do very much good to just stay angry because it saps up too much of your energy."*

SOME MIGHT HAVE called it her "Achillary's Heel," this question on a placard demanding: "Hillary, Who Elected You President?"

It was waiting for her in Lincoln, Nebraska, but could just as easily have been any other place where questions still smoldered about the legality of it, the propriety of it, the wisdom of it, but most of all the audacity of delegating such authority to this other Clinton in the White House.

Never, in the 204-year history of the American presidency, had a chief of state been so quick to publicly acknowledge his reliance on a long-standing political "crony"—even more shocking, in this instance, because it was his wife. Wasn't it just what the right-of-center Cassandras had been prophesying for more than a year? Wasn't the swiftness with which President Bill Clinton assigned her to take on one of the nation's most pressing problems—health care reform—just one more bit of evidence that this was indeed an arrogant, pushy "broad" with an agenda of her own? Who was the real Hillary Rodham Clinton and wasn't it about time that she leveled with the public about what exactly she was up to?

Those, though, were not the questions two thousand people were wrestling with at the University of Nebraska that wintry April day in 1993. Theirs focused on a subject far more pressing than political philosophy: health care and how to revamp it. Not to find the answers, Hillary told them, almost certainly would mean "skyrocketing costs" that would double by the end of the century or, worse still, price health care right out of existence for most people. Senator Bob Kerrey, who recently had changed his mind about whether Hillary was the best person to run Bill Clinton's task force on health care reform, had only praise for the courage it took for her "to bring the nation's attention to this issue."

For Hillary, the "issue" of health care had troubled her long before she ever reached the White House. She had worked to improve it—supporting childhood immunizations and better access to care for rural areas—throughout her husband's five terms as governor and before that as a student activist forming the beliefs that would shape her destiny as a leading advocate for children's rights. This time, however, the health care issue took on a personal dimension. Her father, victim of a stroke in late March, had lain suspended between life and death for three weeks in a Little Rock hospital. All the complex ethical, philosophical and theological questions pertaining to a life-threatening illness, which thousands of families faced every day, had demanded answers from Hillary and her family.

The day before Hugh Rodham died, Hillary touched on those compelling verdicts by calling for "a new ethos of individual responsibility and caring" in a speech to a University of Texas audience of more than ten thousand people, including Lady Bird Johnson and Texas Governor Ann Richards.

"When does life start; when does life end?" Hillary asked. "Who makes those decisions? How do we dare to impinge upon these areas of such delicate, difficult questions? And yet, every day in hospitals and homes and hospices all over this country, people are struggling with those very profound issues . . . issues that we have to summon up what we believe is morally and ethically and spiritually correct and do the best we can with God's guidance. How do we create a system that gets rid of the micromanagement, the regulation and the bureaucracy, and substitutes instead human caring, concern and love?"

"That," she said, "is our real challenge in redesigning a health care system."

That—a moral world where people cared about one another—was what Hillary Clinton believed in.

Health care. It had been right up at the top of Bill Clinton's priorities, along with "help with education," "the forgotten middle class" and "the American

Dream," when he announced in October 1991 that he was running for president. The underlying theme of the campaign he was about to launch—change—would be one Hillary had sounded that summer morning in the kitchen at the Governor's Mansion.

What struck David Wilhelm, the Chicago-based political consultant who became Bill Clinton's campaign manager, in his first meeting with the Clintons was that not once did they talk about campaign strategy or how to prepare for the New Hampshire primary. "We talked public policy the whole time," said Wilhelm. "I remember thinking of Hillary, 'This is a person whose purpose in politics is issues.' " The Clintons' campaign and the decision to run had always been about "something bigger," according to Wilhelm, and that something proved to be the glue "that kept all of us together in pretty tough times."

What fueled uneasiness about Hillary throughout the campaign had been The Clintons, plural, their two-for-the-price-of-one co-presidency. Even among those supportive of women playing a bigger role in policymaking, Hillary would be a discomfiting presence as she put herself forward to speak, admittedly authoritatively, on issues like health care and children, sometimes saying "my husband" but more often than not using the more ominous-sounding "we."

"She was very impressive, you understand," said Harriett Woods, president of the National Women's Political Caucus and a former U.S. Senate candidate whose own spouse had played a supporting role in 1982, remembering one of the first times she saw Hillary in action at a Washington coffee. "You had the feeling that *she* could be the candidate. At the same time there was this, well, 'Wait a minute! She's standing in for her husband but isn't she pushing her role a little far?' From a nonideological viewpoint, to be confronted with this wife of a candidate who seemed to be usurping the role was very off-putting."

Hillary's passion to make a difference in reshaping public policies and attitudes about children's and family issues, not the least of which was health care, had not lessened in the twenty years since she was at Yale. "I think that trying to bring about the kinds of changes that I think are important is a real gift that I couldn't possibly do anything other than try to fulfill the best way I know how," she told me in an interview.

But it was a passion that as the campaign progressed would bother others to such an extent that it became a point of attack. By late April 1992, voters' reaction to Hillary's latest impolitic remark, this one a seeming indictment of women who stayed home and baked cookies that denoted to critics a deeper contempt, confirmed for Clinton's political consultants that it wasn't just government and society that needed overhauling. It was the image the Clintons projected to voters, Bill as glad-handing and weak and Hillary as power-hungry and obsessed with calling the shots.

Opinionated, maybe, "with the best strategic head you're ever going to run into," according to Betsey Wright. But never a meddler. Put the Clintons together, disagreeing with each other, and there was always the chance of fireworks. "They don't do anything that isn't strongly. Whether it's agree or disagree, it's strongly," Wright said. "They are two of the most passionate people I ever met. They love passionately, they argue passionately, they parent passionately, they read passionately, they play passionately."

Hillary had shown a steely toughness throughout the "bimbo issue," as the media dubbed allegations of Bill Clinton's extramarital affairs. When the *Star*, a racy supermarket tabloid, broke a story in which lounge singer Gennifer Flowers claimed she and Clinton had carried on a twelve-year liaison—and the mainstream press more or less picked up on it—many in the Clinton camp were prepared to fold their tents. "Our smoking bimbo has emerged," David Wilhelm told media consultant Frank Greer.

"I think anybody would be lying to you if they said it always looked like we would remain in the race and the outcome would be what, in fact, it turned out to be," Wilhelm said later. "But in the midst of the Gennifer Flowers stuff, Hillary got on a conference call and read us all the riot act. There were a hundred different messages she could have sent, but she sent the absolute correct message: we're in this; we're in this for a reason that's more than us as individuals; get back to work."

To the Clintons' ambushed troops it showed a mental and emotional strength and commitment at a key moment. "We were hearing from him, too, but it was important to hear from her," said Wilhelm. "I think all of us thought, 'Well, for crying out loud, if Hillary can make it through this then we're all going to have the strength to make it through.'"

In some respects, it may have been harder for the Clintons to watch than to appear on *60 Minutes* a few nights after the Flowers allegations broke. CBS taped the Clintons' interview with Steve Kroft in Boston for airing later that night at the conclusion of the Super Bowl. The delay gave the Clintons time to fly home to Little Rock where, with Chelsea sitting on her father's lap, Bill and Hillary saw the edited segment, a much shorter version than had been promised. Bill had been furious because the most emotional parts had been cut, *Newsweek* later reported. "In retrospect," said Wilhelm, "I think we were angry with ourselves for not negotiating a straight playing of the interview."

What some viewers saw as the most incriminating portions of the interview had not been cut. "Wait a minute, wait a minute, wait a minute," Bill demanded at one point of Steve Kroft, who suggested the Clintons had "reached some sort of an understanding and an arrangement" in staying together: "You're looking at two people who love each other. This is not an arrangement or an understanding; this is a marriage. That's a very different thing."

Added Hillary, in an addendum that would alienate her from yet another constituency and demand yet another apology: "You know, I'm not sitting here as some little woman standing by my man, like Tammy Wynette. I'm sitting here because I love him and I respect him and I honor what he's been through and what we've been through together. And, you know, if that's not enough for people, then, heck, don't vote for him."

And Chelsea? What had this eleven-year-old child thought of these parents who had been preparing her for just such a political contingency throughout half of

her life? The same child who would be protected from
public scrutiny (to such an extent that Hillary had been
"stunned" to find out that people did not know she
and Bill had a child) but never from the realities of life
in a political family? Bill said he asked her what she
thought. "I think I'm glad you're my parents," she
replied.

Behind the scenes, friends from the Clintons' recent and distant past rallied to their support. Clifford
Green, the theologian and ethicist who taught Hillary
Old and New Testament at Wellesley, wrote to com-
mend her for "real integrity but without being trapped
by media prying." Contemplating the question of what
it meant to tell the truth, particularly someone of
international visibility, Green reminded Hillary of an
essay by German theologian Dietrich Bonhoeffer.
While being interrogated in a Nazi prison about his
role in the resistance movement, Bonhoeffer wrote:
"There is a very great difference between truth-telling
and cynical exposure." Green said he wrote that what
happened next would "test the maturity of the electorate and the integrity of the media. Let me know if you
need a one-liner." Scrawled at the end of Hillary's
reply ("I still recognized her handwriting") was "I still
remember our lessons from our Bible classes and even
told a Wellesley audience I wish we hadn't eliminated
the requirement."

David Matthews, who from his home in Arkansas
had watched his old University of Arkansas law professor plummet in the polls, hopped a plane to New
Hampshire. A few days before the primary, he and
other Arkansas Travelers accompanied Clinton on a

walk when reporters and photographers mobbed the candidate and in the jostling for positions a Clinton friend had been hurt. Hillary called it one of the ugliest moments in the campaign. Her resolve to persevere was mixed with sorrow.

"We were back in the hotel room and the only people in the room were Hillary and me," Matthews said. "She looked at me with a kind of sadness and said, 'If I didn't really think that we could make a difference in this country, it wouldn't be worth it.' "

Ahead, though, were less noble moments. Hillary was guaranteed tabloid headlines she could have done without when she sniped to Gail Sheehy for *Vanity Fair* about the media's "double standards" in barely covering a rumored but never substantiated extramarital affair of George Bush. Already reeling from her earlier indiscretions—"You know," Virginia Kelley said in our interview that August, "Hillary has a mind of her own, and I haven't heard her misspeak many times"—she was a definite distraction.

Portrayed as a hard-driving careerist, "I hardly recognized myself," she told *Newsweek*'s Mark Miller. So for the second time in her role as The Candidate's Wife, the push was on to remake her image. Then there was the physical remake, undertaken on California primary day by Hollywood friends who hijacked her to actress Markie Post's San Fernando Valley home ostensibly to see a pilot of *Hearts Afire*, starring Post. When Californians counted their returns that night, Hillary turned up at Bill's victory party in restyled hair and clothes. "She's never been in denial about anything in her life," actress Mary Steenburgen told Susan Watters for *Women's Wear Daily*. "She's way too clever, too straight and too ferociously brave for that. She may not share every truth about her life, thank God! We have that ad nauseum with people willing to spill every gut they've got. She holds on to the deepest part of her life the way any other sane person must do."

By the time the Democrats convened in New York City in July to hand Bill Clinton the nomination, the Hillary whom voters saw was a believably affectionate and sharing partner, and a caring, attentive working mother with whom they could identify and feel comfortable. If Republicans choked on her chocolate chip cookies—she agreed to square off against Barbara Bush in a contest sponsored by a women's magazine—it was, as Republican consultant Roger Ailes observed, because "Hillary Clinton in an apron is like Michael Dukakis in a tank."

Practical pols like Harriett Woods saw "nothing cynical" about rounding off Hillary's sharp corners. "The spouse does whatever is most effective to get the candidate elected," said Woods, who saw the focus on Hillary "revolving not around her style and how she looked but around her own capabilities to make a contribution and how she did it" as a turning point in this country.

The Republicans plotted out their own strategy for dealing with Hillary in Houston. They had Barbara Bush and not much else. The Democrats had the cuddlier Clintons, their newest best friends Tennessee Senator Al Gore, his wife, Tipper, and a month's head start campaigning aboard customized buses to Everywhere USA. Bill and Hill and Al and Tip were America's fun foursome, wives climbing onto the laps of their spouses for the benefit of the caravan's photographers. "This is home away from home," said Hillary. "If we win this thing," said Bill, "we're going to park this bus out behind the White House."

The Clintons and the Gores weren't strangers. Little Rock attorney Mark Grobmyer first introduced them all in 1987 when he was state co-chairman for Gore's short-lived presidential campaign. Grobmyer knew both Clintons from Fayetteville when Hillary ran the legal aid clinic and he was one of her students. By 1992, he had become such a nag about Gore as Bill's running mate that around hole ten at the Chenal Country Club the Sunday before Clinton announced his choice, Bill silenced Grobmyer by telling him: "Well, if we can just play golf and you won't talk about it anymore I might pick him."

Republicans couldn't touch Tipper Gore, the psychology-major stay-at-home mother of four and one of the leaders of the controversial crusade to require the recording industry to label its music for parental guidance. Her 1988 book, *Raising PG Kids in an X-Rated Society*, had not helped Al's bid for the presidency in some quarters of the Democratic Party, but she hadn't budged. "I was right then," she told Julia Reed for *Vogue* in 1992, "I'm right now."

But when the Republicans convened in Houston in late August, they had no compunction about turning Hillary Clinton into a dung heap of all that was wrong with career-crazed feminists in America. Scrambling for a pitchfork was Marilyn Quayle, who argued that "most women do not wish to be liberated from their essential natures as women." She and her husband, Vice President Dan Quayle, were living testimony that not every baby-boomer "demonstrated, dropped out, took drugs, joined in the sexual revolution or dodged the draft," though she failed to mention that her husband, like thousands of other young men coming of age during the Vietnam War, had legally avoided the draft by joining the National Guard. "We learned that commitment, marriage and fidelity are not just arbitrary arrangements," she said, following up on her husband's criticism of the Murphy Browns of modern motherhood.

Barbara Bush heard the speech for the first time like everybody else and "pretty much agreed with what Mrs. Quayle was saying," said Anna Perez, Barbara's press secretary, adding, "she just didn't agree with a couple of ways she said it."

The task of conciliation within the party's ranks seemed to fall to Barbara. Recast in her 1988 smash hit title role as Everybody's Grandmother, she went on prime-time television to remind Americans that to overcome the evils of drugs, promiscuity and violence, families had to be strong. "However you define family," she said, "that's what we mean by family values."

In an interview with reporters a few days earlier at the White House, Barbara had shown a cranky combativeness. She rebuked the media for printing a *New York Post* story—"an unsubstantiated lie in every way, shape or form," she said—that President Bush once had an extramarital affair. She said she did not approve of GOP chairman Richard N. Bond's criticism of Hillary Clinton, whom he said "likened marriage and family to slavery." Barbara later thought better of it and repudiated her disapproval on grounds that she had not known exactly what Bond said. "So I may agree with him . . . I just don't like attacking." That did not apply to her husband, however. No, she said, she would not ask President Bush to refrain from such attacks though she did not deny that he had told a New Jersey audience that his opponents "even encourage kids to hire lawyers and haul their parents into court."

The Republicans' strategy had not worked, however. "Every time they bashed Hillary during that week, her numbers went up," said David Wilhelm. "That was something that was doomed to backfire, that appealed only to haters—and part of the electorate will always be haters. Luckily, you don't need to have the haters to win an election."

Hillary said later she had found it "sad, because they all knew better. It wasn't accurate . . . Mrs. Bush has written a book complimenting the work I've done on behalf of children, including a program I had brought to Arkansas. (Barbara Bush's family literacy handbook, *First Teachers*, published in 1989 by the Barbara Bush Foundation for Family Literacy, cited the Arkansas Home Instruction Program for Preschool Youngsters [HIPPY] as one of the ten leading "pioneering and promising efforts.") As for President Bush, Hillary said he "has written me a note and thanked me for talking to him about things that were important, like infant mortality."

Hillary admitted later she had been angry. "You always get angry when people lie about you, but it doesn't do very much good to just stay angry because it saps up too much of your energy," she said. "You have to do the very best you can every day to give people a chance to get to know you, and to try to refute the things that are said about you. And that's all you can do."

Besides, as she used to say in those stock replies the campaign sent out to overcome voters' doubts, she had *never* had anything against baking.

In Little Rock, when she and Bill woke up the morning of November 4, 1992, they looked at each other and started to laugh. In Washington, D.C., the neighborhood bullies were starting to circle.

Hillary and Bill with Steve Kroft in the *60 Minutes* interview on January 25, 1992, when the Clintons met head-on claims by a Little Rock lounge singer that Bill had been her lover. Hillary angered the country music crowd and singer Tammy Wynette when she said she wasn't sitting there "as some little woman standing by my man, like Tammy Wynette" but was a strong factor in keeping Bill's campaign from self-destructing. (© *Steve Liss/CBS News/SABA*)

A few days before the July 1992 Democratic National Convention opens in New York City, presidential hopeful Bill Clinton ends the guessing game by introducing his running mate, Tennessee Senator Al Gore, at the Arkansas Governor's Mansion. *From left:* Clinton, Hillary, Chelsea Clinton, Kristin Gore, fifteen, Sarah Gore, thirteen, Albert Gore III, nine, Gore's wife, Mary Elizabeth "Tipper" Gore, and vice presidential candidate Al Gore. Not present is a fourth Gore child, Karenna, eighteen. (*Reuters/Bettmann*)

Hillary during happier moments with her parents, Hugh and Dorothy Rodham, at the July 1992 Democratic National Convention in New York City. Less than a year later, Hugh Rodham would suffer a stroke and in his final weeks would bring the heartache of a family illness even closer to the czarina of health care reform, his daughter. *(AP/World Wide Photos)*

Victory! President-elect Bill Clinton waves to the crowd at the Old Statehouse in Little Rock on election night 1992 while Hillary clasps hands with supporters. *At left*: Vice President-elect Al Gore and Tipper Gore reach out to the tumultuous crowd as their children and Chelsea watch from the stage. Behind Clinton are his mother, Virginia, and her husband, Richard Kelley. *(© Rich Lipski/*The Washington Post*)*

Hillary presents Rosalynn Carter the Eleanor Roosevelt Living World Award at a Peace Links banquet in December 1992. Hillary was often compared to the controversial Eleanor, but it was the activist Rosalynn who set the stage for Hillary's redefinition of the role of First Lady. Jimmy Carter, like Bill Clinton, involved his wife in matters of state when he was governor of Georgia and wanted her equally engaged in his presidency. (© *Nancy Andrews*/The Washington Post)

Their husbands had spent months fighting over the White House, and two weeks after the election, the victor's wife looked over his spoils. A gracious Barbara Bush welcomes Hillary before taking her on a tour of the house where she would soon be living. Their campaign rhetoric a thing of the past, Barbara and Hillary show a united front to the media staked out on the South Lawn. "Avoid this crowd like the plague," cautioned Barbara. "And if they quote you, make damn sure they heard you." Nodded Hillary: "That's right. I know that feeling already." (© *James A. Parcell*/The Washington Post)

President and Mrs. Bush greet President-elect and Mrs. Clinton and Chelsea at the White House on January 20, 1993. The mansion's new occupant gives a hail-and-farewell pat to outgoing First Dog Millie whose departure marks the end of the twelve-year-long Canine Era. The Feline Era began ten days later with the arrival of Chelsea's cat Socks (*not pictured*), whose mission would be to reduce the rat population at the White House. (© *Dayna Smith*/The Washington Post)

William Jefferson Clinton becomes America's forty-second president as Chief Justice William H. Rehnquist administers the oath of office on the U.S. Capitol's West Front on Inauguration Day. A solemn Chelsea listens as her father swears to "preserve, protect and defend the Constitution of the United States." Hillary Rodham Clinton said her eyes were nearly blinded by tears of pride she felt for her husband. (© *Ray Lustig*/The Washington Post)

First Lady Hillary Rodham Clinton gives a jaunty thumbs-up to ecstatic Democrats at one of the thirteen Inaugural Balls going on around Washington on Inauguration night. Though president only a few hours, Bill Clinton was already blowing his own horn—his beloved saxophone—at several of the balls attended by some seventy thousand. Hillary wears the glittering violet Inaugural Ball gown created for her by Sarah Phillips, up until then an unknown New York designer. Her French twist hairdo was yet another variation of the coiffeurs Hillary has tried out. (© *Lucian Perkins*/The Washington Post)

Earning a place in presidential lore as Smoke-Free Hillary—and presumably on the tobacco industry's hate list—the new First Lady deep-sixed ashtrays around the mansion, announcing that smoking would no longer be permitted in the White House. Here, beneath the portrait of Abraham Lincoln and wearing a Donna Karan shoulderless dress, she inspects table arrangements in the State Dining Room for the Clintons' first official black-tie dinner, honoring the nation's governors, on January 31, 1993. In her first post-Inaugural interview, Hillary told *New York Times* writer Marian Burros the health issue was so important to her that she didn't think smoking should be allowed in the president's house any longer. There was no smoke but there was definitely fire from the rest of the media furious over being scooped. Their complaints fell on deaf ears, however. The First Lady continued to be methodically selective about whom she did and did not talk to, and when. *(© Suzanne De Chillo/*New York Times *Pictures)*

Hillary (*right*) listens as the president (*not shown*) introduces her as Hillary Rodham Clinton, chairman of the Presidential Task Force on National Health Care Reform. The announcement confirms that she is his closest advisor and reasserting her own identity. For the next six hours she telephoned influential members of Congress, some hailing her appointment as a way of expediting national health care policy, others less enthusiastic about a president's wife having so powerful an assignment. *From left:* in foreground, Laura Tyson, Council of Economic Advisors chairman, Secretary of Health and Human Services Donna Shalala, Hillary's old Children's Defense Fund ally and senior White House policy advisor Ira Magaziner. *(© Rich Lipski/*The Washington Post*)*

Hillary and Senate Majority Leader George J. Mitchell brief the press on her Capitol Hill session with thirty Democratic senators to discuss health care reform. Afterward, she paid a courtesy call on Senate Minority Leader Robert J. Dole. He called her Hillary, but when word got back that she called him Bob, Dole was asked if her informality bothered him. Replied Dole: "Last time I checked that was my name." *(© Larry Morris/*The Washington Post)

Hillary sees key Democrats in the House, in another get-acquainted visit to sound out congressional leaders on health care reform. Here, she and Speaker Tom Foley (*right*) defer to Majority Leader Richard A. Gephardt. A few days later, Hillary is sued by health industry groups contending that since she is not a federal employee her task force meetings must be held in public. The judge rules in the plaintiffs' favor. *(© Ray Lustig/*The Washington Post)

Betty Ford pitches provisions for mental health and substances abuse in health care reform during a two-hour visit with Hillary in March 1993. In becoming First Lady, Hillary joined the most exclusive "sorority" in the country—the collegial ranks of seven women whose husbands were U.S. presidents. Once campaign cheering and booing stops, first ladies traditionally close ranks despite their partisan ties. Nobody knows better than they the pressures and strains of fishbowl living. (© *Rich Lipski*/The Washington Post)

Hillary, with former First Lady Lady Bird Johnson and Texas Governor Ann Richards in Austin the day before Hugh Rodham died. In a roundtable discussion at the University of Texas on "Remodeling Our Society," Hillary turns philosophical and provides a rare glimpse into her spiritual nature, which fortified her throughout other difficult times in her life and laid the foundation of her moral and ethical beliefs as a child. (*Reuters/Bettmann*)

Hillary gave a One Hundred Days party for her staff at the White House the night before this photograph was taken on May 1, 1993. Flying back from the University of Michigan in Ann Arbor, the First Lady couldn't decide which of her dresses would photograph better that night at the White House Correspondents Association dinner. Rather than dark, she chose white, giving her an almost ethereal quality, a look some believe suggested a "Saint Hillary." (© *Frank Johnston*/The Washington Post)

Hillary's hair provided endless media attention. "I figure that if we ever want to get Bosnia off the front page all I have to do is either put on a headband or change my hair and we'll be occupied with something else," she joked in April 1993. But she was wrong. President Clinton unwittingly upstaged her with his new hairdo a month later, about the same time that Hillary appeared in public with this new style by Frederic Fekkai of New York City. (© *Harry Naltchayan*/The Washington Post)

# 11

## A Place
of
## Her Own

*"You have to try to stand for something bigger
than yourself."*

JOHN KENNEDY SCATTERED the seeds of the Peace Corps there in 1960. Lyndon Johnson rooted the Great Society there in 1965. George Bush, as part of his "vision thing," called for a "Good Society" there in 1991 because "We don't need another '*Great* Society' with huge and ambitious programs administered by the incumbent few. We need a '*Good* Society,' " he told a crowd of sixty-eight thousand, ". . . built upon the needs of the many."

Here, now, in the shadow of these presidents on a brilliant first day of May, stood Hillary Rodham Clinton—or as her fourth and newest honorary Doctorate of Laws identified her in Latin, "Hillarium Rodham Clinton." She was a small but authoritative figure in her billowy black gown of academia, elevating "good" to "excellence" for 6,500 students receiving degrees at this colossus of American higher education, the University of Michigan at Ann Arbor. "Your excellence is not only about you, but it is about your generation and your country," she told them. "Excellence is not found in any single moment in our lives. It is not about those who shine always in the sun or those who fail to succeed in the darkness of human error or mistake. It is about who we are, what we believe in, what we do with every day of our lives."

Overhead, a small plane scudded across the cloudless sky trailing a banner—"Equal Rights for Unborn First Ladies" on one go-round, "College for the Unborn, Too; Impeach Hillary," on another. The crowd of fifty thousand noticed; Hillary, who will likely go nowhere during her tenure in the White House without criticism from somewhere, appeared unperturbed. Not that dissent much bothered her in any form. Twenty-four years earlier when she was the student speaker at her own Wellesley College commencement, she had voiced her own dissent about a wounded society, a society in which "the divisions of the Vietnam era and the combustible mix of racism and poverty that exploded in so many of our cities" had enraged a generation.

"Going back and reading it now I see the idealism," she continued, her amplified voice resonating around the huge Michigan stadium. "I see the excitement and I know that at twenty-one I was perhaps unable to appreciate the political and social restraint that one faces in the world. But I'm glad I felt like that when I was twenty-one, and I have always tried to keep those feelings with me. I want to be idealistic, I want to care about the world, I want to be connected to other people."

Idealism and restraint. A deep belief in the need to reform the system yet a reverence for the rules of that system, rules that impeded reform. The dichotomy of Hillary Clinton was on display that afternoon as clearly as any time since she had first swept into the national consciousness not much more than a year before and since she had remade the job of First Lady starting 102 days earlier.

Amid the cheers, Hillary, The Pragmatist, was also reminding young listeners that while the Cold War was over and minorities and women had greater rights than when she was their age, "society was too often coming apart instead of coming together." New problems demanded the "right balance," equalizing rights with responsibility and learning "what you are willing to stand for and stand against." It wasn't enough to promote the common good and provide each other with certain rights and opportunities if people weren't "responsible to themselves for themselves and on behalf of their families."

Later, she slumped into her seat aboard the Air Force C-9 jet taking her back to Washington, admitting she was exhausted by her own One Hundred Days—the seven-day weeks, sixteen-hour days mostly in pursuit of a plan to reform the nation's health care system and a method to sell it to the public—and by the bedside vigil she had kept of her dying father. She considered more heavily the "political and social restraint" one faced as a forty-five-year-old whose balancing act of personal duty and public commitment no other First Lady in history had undertaken. Remembering that "wonderful old aphorism"—Winston Churchill's—that "a man who is not a liberal at twenty has no heart, and one who is not a conservative at forty has no head," she said she was "trying to recognize what is the obvious reality of how difficult change is, but with the deep feeling I have that you have to stay engaged, stay committed."

With so many centers of influence demanding to be heard—from the media and culture, to government and big business and everyone in between—it was difficult figuring out how to get results you could believe in. "If you worry as I do about what happens in our inner city, that's not just a political issue," she said, "that's a family issue, a cultural issue, an educational issue, the changing economic fortunes of people." Still, while you had to recognize the complexities, you couldn't let them beat you down. "A lot of people are cynical," she said, "because out of their former idealism they can't keep their energy levels up in the face of problems that seem so intractable."

Hillary, herself, can be cautious, vigilant and wary, but never cynical. Having run the gauntlet of distortions, skepticism and smears on everything from her politics to her sexuality, the girl who had learned at an early age to stand up to the neighborhood bullies had made it through her first trials with Washington bullies scarred but sound. Now she was just weeks away from stepping back into the arena in a way that likely would make insignificant so many of her prior public missions. She was preparing to put herself before the country, and all its warring factions, as the chief salesman of the Clinton administration's intricate, ambitious and wholly untested scheme to reorder 14 percent of the American economy, otherwise known as health care reform. She knew that even as she refined her own strategy, forces of self-interest from the health care industry were preparing to pick at her with a ferocity that would make the bullies of Park Ridge, Illinois, seem like Girl Scouts.

She pushed aside the Clinton-era taco salad that had replaced the Bush-era beans and weenies and the Reagan-era seafood salad on the menu of Executive One, so named when the First Lady was aboard. "Actually," she said, "I feel more energized because I think all of us are beginning to understand Washington better and get a more realistic sense of how it works. I have a clearer idea in my own mind about what it'll take to make these arguments that will change the government's direction. The problems are not quite as overwhelming and undefined as when we started off our agenda for change. I feel liberated."

"Liberated" might seem short of the mark for this highly conspicuous First Lady already tagged "First Adviser to the President." "I wish we wouldn't have to reinvent history all the time, that we could do away with the stereotypes of what is or is not," Hillary said. Defining it even as she performed it, her version of The Role was daring and powerful—and to her critics worrisome, considering that eight, twelve or sixteen years hence a woman in the highest office of the land might seem as safe a bet as a man. Hillary Rodham

Clinton, now forty-five, would still be a woman of a very acceptable certain age.

Despite his once-passionate talk of activism and purpose, President Clinton had ended his first hundred days blandly disconnected. With ill-timed naïveté he had launched his presidency in a toe-to-toe confrontation with Washington's resident resisters: the Joint Chiefs of Staff over ending the ban on gays in the military, the revenge-seeking Republicans determined to show him Pennsylvania Avenue was a two-way street, and the ingrained layers of lobbyists protecting their special turfs. Meanwhile, the puzzled American public watched the show much as they might a silent movie of botched starts and spliced restarts, trying to keep the story line straight if only they could read his lips. For all Hillary's vulnerabilities, she was the one who came across as directed and convincing, far more effective at putting their message across. They had always complemented each other, so superbly trading off strengths for shortcomings that they were far better together than apart. Said one friend of the partnership: "There wouldn't be a Bill Clinton without a Hillary."

So while Bill Clinton floundered, Hillary flourished as the cool-headed, rational, far-sighted harbinger of change. To her supporters—both men and women—she was the best role model women ever had going for them, the symbol of their changing status in society but also the agent of change. She was truly a First Lady of her time, arriving at a point in history when people were ready for her. And as events had played out, she was not only the beneficiary of change but the precursor of change.

Not at all sure of the ground rules, Washington's resident power structure—the unarguably male movers—had struggled with how to deal with her, just as the nation's media—the unarguably male shakers—had wrestled with how to cover her. Pitting the traditionalists against the barrier-breakers, the debate ricocheted between such threatening prospects as whether she would be a "policymaker," have an office in the West Wing near the President's Oval Office or impose her professional skills at the White House as she had in the marketplace for nearly twenty years. The more compelling question among women, though, was how Hillary could avoid wasting her considerable talent, ability and experience on the trivia of First Ladydom.

The truth of the matter was that beyond the traditional tasks of wife, hostess and helpmate, first ladies never had any safe role to play. The bullies had always been around. Certainly, there was nothing safe about the trailblazing activism of Eleanor Roosevelt, whose political clout was so potent that an FDR crony once told her that if she wanted to be president in 1940, she should tell him so he could start getting things ready.

Hillary was intrigued by Eleanor, who held an unsalaried job in FDR's wartime administration, as deputy director of the Office of Civilian Defense, and throughout his thirteen years as president took enormous flak in her fight against racism, sexism and poverty. During the 1992 campaign, Hillary said she didn't let criticism bother her but later confessed she used to carry on an imaginary conversation with Eleanor, whom she had never met, asking advice on how to put up with the attacks and criticism she was encountering. The answer would always be: "Get out and do it, and don't make any excuses about it."

By the 1960s, first ladies were expected to take on more activist roles, but their "causes" were necessarily uncontroversial. Pat Nixon veered away from job training and adult education in the sphere of social welfare, allying herself with "volunteerism" after her husband took office. Less concerned about political fallout was the independent-thinking Betty Ford, who threw the power of her White House pulpit behind women's rights, in general, and the Equal Rights Amendment, in particular.

Wives of presidential candidates who did not have a cause could always invent one. When I asked Margot Perot at the height of her husband's boomlet in 1992 what her cause would be, she asked what I thought it *should* be. Barbara Bush made no bones of the fact that she knew she needed a cause if George ran for president in 1980. She had hit upon family literacy after listening to his experts assess domestic problems. Long before family values became a campaign war cry, she believed that if more people could read and write, there would be fewer problems with drugs and violence and unwanted pregnancies. Despite their rhetoric, Barbara had won Hillary's regard for doing "the very best job she could with the way she defined her life. I respect her for the choices she made," Hillary told me in Cleveland during the campaign.

Nancy Reagan had shown some interest in drug abuse when Ronald Reagan was governor of California but not until her negative ratings imperiled her husband's effectiveness in dealing with the economy was her Say-No-to-Drugs campaign launched a year after Ronald Reagan became president. Although she was determined to eliminate the stigma and incidence of mental illness and eventually made good on her campaign "promise" to have Congress enact a President's Commission on Mental Health, Rosalynn Carter drew scant attention from the media for her efforts. But her unforgivable sin had not been a cause at all, only that that she was ahead of her time, strong-willed, goal-oriented, perceived as "Mom" to Jimmy's "Pop" and trying to run the store they lived above.

Twelve years after Jimmy lost, Rosalynn remained baffled by America's ambivalence over the role of the First Lady. "Americans know that women are going to work," she said of the controversy Hillary touched off. "They don't mind if women work. They think it's nice for women to have leadership positions—I think they really do—but they think the First Lady ought to sit in the White House and take care of the president. I cannot understand that. I told Hillary, 'You're going to be criticized no matter what you do, so be criticized for what you think is best and right for the country.' "

Hillary had done just that. In Cleveland a few days before the election, she had talked about the "job" that had no description, no mandate, no paycheck. "What I hope is that each woman, and someday men in that position, will be free to be who they are," she said. "If that means being a full-time career person not involved in the issues of the day but very much wrapped up in his or her own career, that should be a choice that we respect. If it's a more traditional role in which the primary focus is in supporting the family that is there and the person who holds the office, *that* is the position we should respect. If it is a more active public role, then I think we ought to be very happy about that."

Nothing had happened since then to change her mind or her choice of the third option. Weary but contemplative as she sat in the same seat where Barbara Bush and Nancy Reagan once sat on trips to sell their causes, she told me she could relate to many of her predecessors' problems. Critical to her was "how I make the right balance between all the different duties I feel I have. I'm very conscious of the social and hostess responsibilities—I did the same thing in Arkansas and actually I like it. I like being able to bring people together and entertain them and enjoy their company. But at the same time, I have the need to do something I feel is important, like this health care issue that goes beyond the accepted duties of the First Lady."

And indeed by that point, a little more than three months into the Clinton administration, the "hostess" side of the job seemed to have been ignored. Ten days after Clinton took office he and Hillary gave a black-tie dinner for the nation's governors but after that, other than some pro forma teas and receptions, including one for foreign presidents and prime ministers when the Holocaust Museum opened, there had been no sign of much presidential entertaining. Missing from action were the ceremonial dinners for foreign leaders. Instead, they came and went at the White House in almost revolving-door fashion. As it appeared to the Washington Establishment, which kept track of such things, this was a decidedly unsocial administration.

Clearly, Hillary's priorities were on policy matters, not politicking—as White House socializing invariably amounted to—and she gave every indication that she intended to go right ahead doing what she thought was right. "That's all I can do. You could literally spend your entire life in a position like this worrying about what other people are thinking about you, and you are never satisfied. I'm more interested in being part of helping to change our country, which is what I care about."

Graduates and their families in Ann Arbor had heard what she cared about this particular day—the National Service program President Clinton announced the day before and, always, health care. It was the ultimate exercise in idealism and pragmatism, in crafting novel solutions to help the greatest number of people and then bending the political process to implement them. It's just that the job was enormous beyond belief. Already in the three prior months, Hillary's health care road show had played in nine states at countless symposiums and sent her to Capitol Hill for more than fifty meetings. And she had barely started.

In Arkansas, she had taken on education reform at her own suggestion. Had she done the same thing with health care? Had she volunteered or been nominated to oversee the five-hundred-member task force? "Wellll, nominated," she ventured cautiously and not entirely convincingly. Once designated, she went about it with the same lawyerly approach she always

used when devising a program that provided her husband with concluding options, and according to those
who know them, almost certainly her own recommendations. On one level, she made certain the factual
information from often conflicting sources was as precise as possible so that policy decisions could be rooted
in more accurate assumptions. On a second level, she
focused on the various policy options and what the
economic projections would mean for each one.

She might not agree one hundred percent with
the decision Bill Clinton ended up making, but her
job, as she saw it, was to give him the best basis for
making his decision. Whatever they—and here she
used the plural pronoun—came up with was likely to
make a lot of people uneasy, just as education reform
had in Arkansas. If, however, everything could be
explained well and if they could show convincingly
that the changes would be good for most Americans,
then they would be ready to take it to the public. It
meant making sure all the steps were right, then being
in a position to explain.

She said the political risks didn't concern her.
What she worried about was "overcoming the inertia
and the extraordinary power of people who want to
keep things just as they are . . . this ideological block-
ade against reality and all these people who basically
think things are fine." Even weeks after hearing about
health care in the real world of ordinary Americans,
Hillary's mental screen was so sharp that she could still
put images with the stories. "I'm convinced that on
some of the trips we have introduced some of the senators and congressmen to the first people they ever met

without health care who worked," she said. "They don't run 'movies' like I do of all these faces, these people."

No one was inclined to doubt her when she said that merely seeking ways to reform the massive health care industry was "the hardest thing I ever tried to do." And that was before she tried to sell anything. But as in so many ventures in her life, the road cleared once she saw the moral focus of what she was trying to accomplish. On a trip to Montana shortly after her father's death, two months into the project, it occurred to her that winning a consensus on health care reform might just be what it took to change America into a "caring" country. "After all," she told Melanne Verveer, her deputy chief of staff, "health care is with us at those most human of moments—the birth of a child, the death of a loved one."

Hillary had taken time out from her life to be there with her eighty-two-year-old father when a stroke felled him in late March. In the two weeks preceding that most final of human moments, she had put health care on hold to be by his bedside. Glimpses of her between hospital and car showed the toll of universal truths about what it means to lose a loved one. Later, in a revealing speech at the University of Texas, she articulated those truths into questions about the individual and collective meaning "at some core level" in life. "We are, I think, in a crisis of meaning," she said.

Unknown in advance even by her staff, which had been expecting a speech about children, Hillary had reached into the little notebook of sayings she carries with her to find the oddly similar thoughts of two profoundly disparate people: Lee Atwater, the "bare-knuckle" architect of Ronald Reagan and George Bush victories, and Albert Schweitzer, the doctor who recognized the "sleeping sickness of soul" as well as of the body. "The most dangerous aspect is that one is unaware of its coming," said Schweitzer. Said Atwater, who died of cancer: "My illness helped me to see that what was missing in society is what was missing in me. A little heart, a lot of brotherhood." While raising questions about when life starts and when it ends, she also asked for a "new politics of meaning . . . a new ethos of individual responsibility and caring . . . a new definition of civil society which answers the unanswerable questions posed by both the market forces and the governmental ones, as to how we can have a society that fills us up again and makes us feel that we are part of something bigger than ourselves."

In the intellectual detective story of who is Hillary Rodham Clinton and what does she believe, the speech was to be a major clue. Her friends had always known about her spiritual quest but the death of her father on the eve of the health care challenge seemed to provide new meaning. Still, just as religion had defined Hillary's life, and change had provided the direction hers took, politics had shaped it ever since her Goldwater Girl days. She was a political enigma to many, not easily explained in liberal-conservative terms.

"I'm part of a growing group of people who want to get beyond those labels," she said to the question, stiffening ever so slightly. "They are so undescriptive anymore that I don't think they easily fit most situations. They are an excuse for not thinking through problems, so that on lots of issues I'm conservative but on other issues I'm liberal. On most issues I'm somewhere in the middle trying to figure out how to get beyond all that. And it's amusing to me that some people are just intent on trying to label me and capture me and then make all these assumptions about what I therefore must believe because they put me in their box. I mean, I don't understand the need for doing that, but it's a big sport, apparently."

In some instances, she had simply outgrown the "box." From the vantage point of the White House, where new ideals have a way of colliding with old realities, even an old nemesis could look different. When Richard Nixon dropped in to see Bill Clinton one day in early March and Hillary and Chelsea stopped by to meet him, they found him "conversational and gracious." A few weeks earlier on NBC's *Today*, he had been "very complimentary of me," said Hillary, obviously pleased. Whatever Nixon's intent had been a year earlier in predicting that Hillary's independence would politically damage her husband, he was a paragon of support when he told Katie Couric that it was "very appropriate" for Hillary to do what she believed to be "the right thing. For example, if she can come up with a solution on health care, then I say we're all for it."

Of course Nixon, the mythic enemy of most 1960s reformers, had also been part of the Hillary Myth. Conservatives who tried to trace her political evolution pointed to the fact that she had worked as an attorney on the impeachment inquiry staff drawing up articles that would have brought Nixon to trial as further proof of a lockstep liberal mentality. Yet in her interview with me, Hillary said she never had "a personal animosity" toward Nixon. "I've always said I thought Richard Nixon absolutely made the right decision for the country by resigning and sparing the country a trial in the Senate and all the anguish that would have produced." Unlike some of her impeachment staff colleagues who had been outraged when Gerald Ford pardoned Nixon, denying the country a definitive ending to the question of his culpability, Hillary believed resigning was sufficient. "That was humiliating and profoundly painful to him. I don't think it would have served any purpose to the country to have continued his agony of allegations of misdoing that rose out of Watergate. I think it was absolutely right to get on with the life of the country."

Contemplating Nixon from the loftiness of thirty thousand feet and the mellowing of time, she saw him as "someone who had very serious conflicts within himself. He did a lot of things that were very significant—the Legal Services Corporation, for example, which is something I care about—so that like most people he had very complex kinds of attitudes." And if he and Lyndon Johnson were oppositive influences in her life, particularly as they pertained to Vietnam, she charitably offered "no doubt that both believed they were doing the right thing. I don't think we were dealing with people who were seeking personal or pecuniary or even, to some extent, political advantage so much as they were overwhelmed by circumstances and brought to those circumstances certain mind-sets and experiences that pushed them in the direction of making decisions that were, in my perspective, wrong because they were not in tune with what was going on at the moment in terms of challenges to America."

The lessons to be learned from that, she said, were "to always ask yourself: 'Am I seeing this problem, whatever it might be, from the prism of my own experience and therefore am I not really open to looking at it in other ways? And blocking information that might be painful or contradictory?' And it's one of the lessons, really, that my husband has taught me because a lot of people say that my husband takes too much information and all that. But when it comes to big things, and when it comes to difficult things, I think it's important to take in a lot of information and to seek out contrary information where that's possible. To look at Presidents Johnson and Nixon, both of whom had good domestic policies, from my perspective, you have to ask yourself how to make sure you don't get caught in those kinds of experience traps."

Speaking earlier at Ann Arbor about "new problems—places with names like Bosnia and Somalia that I never heard of when I graduated from college," Hillary might have been thinking that her husband could be facing his own "experience trap." Even as she was flying back to the White House, he was closeted with key foreign affairs advisors on whether to use military force against the Serbs in Bosnia-Herzegovina. Already there were warnings that if he sent in bombers or, worse, ground troops, this "Southeast Asia of Europe" could become his own Vietnam.

For all the time she spent on and off Capitol Hill

as a college intern and later as a young lawyer on the impeachment inquiry staff, she said she never really had the total take on how things worked there. Much of what she had learned about dealing with Congress had come out of her recent meetings with its powerful members. She had earned a grudging respect from them and the media. Rather than a resistance, as some critics had predicted, she characterized her reception by "these older men as a kind of bewilderment, a suspension of judgment" that in time turned into real support by some members and at least a "level of courtesy" by others.

At least initially, Hillary had an easier time adjusting to Washington than her husband in large part because she had never been reticent about asking questions or searching for new meaning in life. She took to the town with the enthusiasm of a wide-eyed newcomer, but undergirded by a rock-solid self-awareness. She had the optimism to believe that every problem had a solution and the self-confidence to think she was the one who could find it. The pieces that had built Hillary—the people, the ideas, the experiences—were all coming together.

The flight was nearly over but not the day. Still ahead was the White House Correspondents' annual dinner, the Clintons' first as First Couple, and it occurred to Hillary that she didn't know what to wear. Should it be something light or something dark, something short or something long? "Dark," said an aide. "Short," said another. There was a suggestion of a frown and then the realization hit Hillary that she was in control. "I can wear what I want," she laughed.

Actually, she had always been in control of her life, and she reflected about that as the plane sped through the nothingness of the atmosphere.

People, for instance. She had a vast network of friends, colleagues and associates. And she had been as acquisitive of them as other people could be of material things. "I sought them out," she said. "I wanted to be around people who were trying to do what I only talked about, with respect to helping people help themselves, changing conditions destructive to children particularly. . . . I always believed you could learn something from nearly everybody you meet, if you're open to it. And depending upon who you're around and who you surround yourself with, who you want to be around."

And then there were Dorothy and Hugh Rodham, her mother and father who throughout her life had never once put up barriers for her and whose styles and parenting skills had always complemented each other.

"My father was like the ambassador from the outside world—'life is hard out there'—all the time encouraging me and never making any distinction based on gender. My father never said, 'I don't think girls should do that.' Or, 'That's not appropriate for a young lady'—all those signals that get sent to girls. He used to say, 'I may not always like what you do but I will always love you.' And when I was a little girl, I used to say, 'Do you mean if I murdered somebody you'd still love me?' And he'd say, 'Yes, I would not approve of what you did, I would be very sad, but I will always love you.' "

Her mother, a relentless self-challenger with "a great spirit of resilience and caring about people," would be the one who stayed up late helping Hillary with her homework, making certain she finished what had to be finished and always being there, always filled with good ideas. "You can't replace that kind of drop-dead stability," said Hillary. "It's just the best parents can give."

Children and parents are perhaps the best example of how the life of Hillary shaped the policy of Hillary. It was the absence in so many American families of that very kind of stability that had troubled Hillary ever since voluntarily baby-sitting for children of mi-grant families working on farms outside Park Ridge. "You have to begin to instill in people some sense of responsibility for themselves and others, and particu-larly adults for children. And go back to some of the tried and true basic ways that we know work better for them. Children need the right combination of atten-tion and discipline and love. And there are too many who are being pushed into growing up too fast and being left to their own devices too early."

She said there were no hard and fast rules about mothers who work. "I think if we were more supportive of mothers from the very beginning, if we had not seen our standard of living decrease so that two people in a family have to work in order to remain in the middle class, if we didn't have so many family breakups so that single mothers are the sole source of support for their families, a lot more women would be able to choose to stay home and be full-time caretakers of their children." There would always be those who did not for whatever combination of reasons. But then in Hillary's view, "they have to take full responsibility for making sure their child is well cared for and given the kind of attention the child needs. We don't do very much to support women in making that choice."

She had talked about that at some length in Cleveland. What she wanted for all women, not just the spouse of a president, was the opportunity for each to make the choices right for herself at various stages of her life. "Because that, too, changes over time. We're all going to be given different opportunities with respect to the time we wish to spend rearing children, or having a career or balancing both. And we ought to do away with any kind of stereotypical expectations and instead celebrate the choices that are finally available to us."

And what of Hillary as First Mom?

"Well, I don't go out unless I absolutely have to," she said. "I try to be home when she's home in the afternoon, or at least talk to her, have dinner with her, help her with her homework. It's been a difficult move for her, too, leaving all her friends behind, her grandfather dying, living in the White House with all that attention, which I don't understand and she sure doesn't."

Suddenly, you had the idea that it just might work out for Hillary Rodham Clinton. And the reason? She had to help Chelsea with her homework. Unlike so many people who went to Washington chasing a single carrot, Hillary Clinton had gone there to live her life, the life she had built block by block from almost the first moment she could build anything. She didn't have the luxury of putting the pieces of her existence into separate boxes, to be opened only on her command. Her life was integrated. The mother, the wife, the activist, the politician, the moralist—they were all in one big box that got opened every day.

"The danger in any kind of a capital city or any governmental activity when you've got power," she said as Executive One started its descent somewhere over Maryland, "is that the sense of mission, contribution and service get mixed up, and pretty soon people start going through motions. The pressures that knock you around all the time can undermine your sense of direction, your integrity as a person and even who you are.

"In the world in which I'm living now, there is so much emphasis on the short term and the secular, I feel really grateful to have some sense of faith and rooting that goes beyond that. And to be reminded," she said, Andrews Air Force Base coming up quickly now, "that you have to try to stand for something bigger than yourself."

# Index

Abortion, 162
Abshire, David, 73
Acheson, Dean, 58, 83
Acheson, Eleanor Dean, 58, 60, 80
Adams, Ruth, 66, 68, 75, 79, 80
Ailes, Roger, 234
Alinsky, Saul, 75, 78
Altshuler, Fred H., 123, 135
American Civil Liberties Union, 92
Anthony, Beryl, 168, 169
Arkansas, 13–16, 32, 105, 127–28, 133–55 *passim*, 171–72, 182, 188–89, 191, 192, 201–13 *passim*
Arkansas Advocates for Children and Families, 166, 180
Armstrong, Bob, 117

Baker, Gerald E., 26–28, 51–52
Ball, Karen, 142
Baroody, William, 73
Bassett, Woody, 138
Bayh, Birch, 163
Bellavance, Russell, 106
Benzinger, Rosalie, 43, 46
Bernstein, Carl, 116
Bickel, Alexander M., 91
Black Panthers, 87, 91, 92, 93

Blacks, 32
civil rights movement, 63
in Park Ridge (Ill.), 46, 47
revolutionaries, 87, 91
at Wellesley, 58, 68–69, 75–76
work of Martin Luther King, 48–49
Blair, Diane, 15, 133–35, 139–48 *passim*, 193, 194, 203–4, 209
Blair, James, 15–16, 193
Blythe, William, 29–30, 174
Boggon, Brian, xix
Bond, Richard N., 236–37
Bonhoeffer, Dietrich, 44, 232
Bosnia, 257
Bowen, Otis, 158
Branch, Taylor, 111–14, 116, 124, 127
Branson, Johanna, 68
Brewster, Kingman, 89, 91, 92
Brooke, Edward, 59–60, 80, 81, 82
Brown, Jerry, 217
Bucknell, Susan, 102
Burros, Marian, 33, 80, 165, 174, 182, 196, 197, 204
Bush, Barbara, 7, 234, 236–37, 248
Bush, George, 219, 233, 236, 237, 241

Califano, Joe, 97
Cambodia, 94
Campbell, Joan, 186
Carmichael, Stokely, 63
Carter, Jimmy, 155–64 *passim,*
   169, 182, 188, 249
Carter, Rosalynn, 249
*Catcher in the Rye,* 45, 47–48
CBS Television, 116
Child and Family Services Act,
   97
Children, 95–98, 102–4, 117–19,
   166, 168, 173, 216, 219, 229,
   237, 260–61
Children's Defense Fund, 118,
   216
Christianity, 17, 44, 48
Churchill, Winston, 244
Civil rights, 63, 67, 70, 81, 92,
   120
Clayton, Patricia Rodham, xvii
Clift, Eleanor, 174
Clinton, Bill (William Jefferson)
  ambitions, 113, 114, 115, 118,
   164, 216
  Arkansas tax increase, 209–11
  attorney general campaign,
   149, 155, 164
  "bimbo" issue, 230
  brother Roger, 214–15
  childhood, 215
  congressional campaign, 127,
   135, 137, 144, 145
  criticism of, 184
  and education reform, 201–13
   *passim,* 219
  and female groupies, 187–88
  first hundred days, 246
  and Gore, 235
  governorship, 171, 182–83,
   188, 204
  and Hillary, 102, 127
  on Hillary, 101, 134, 203
  Hillary on, 11, 101, 102

  loss of governorship, 188–91
  marital problems, 185–86
  on marriage, 231
  McGovern campaign, 111,
   114–17
  meeting of Hillary, 100
  meeting of Hillary's mother,
   104–5
  1988 election, 218–19
  presidential aspirations, 221–22
  as product of Arkansas schools,
   206
  religion, 191
  on Rodhams, 144
  salary, 164
  *60 Minutes* interview, 186,
   230–31
  victory speech, 18–19
  at Yale, 99–100, 102, 106
Clinton, Chelsea, 4, 10, 196, 261
  birth, 174–75
  coaching by parents, 218
  grandmother's influence, 197
  as infant, 181
  naming of, 174
  on parents, 231–32
Clinton, Hillary Rodham
  activism, 59
  on Alinsky, 78
  and Arkansas, 127–28, 133,
   136–37, 139–40, 143–45,
   147, 202
  as Arkansas First Lady,
   171–72, 217, 220
  awards, 56, 213
  on Bill, 11, 101, 102, 219
  Bill on, 101
  and "bimbo" issue, 230
  birth, 29
  birth of Chelsea, 174–75, 179,
   181–82
  career, 130, 146, 149, 195–96
  and Carter campaign, 156–64,
   169

childhood, 30–31, 33–36
children's issues, 96–98, 102–4,
    117–19, 166, 168, 173, 216,
    219, 229, 237, 260–61
chocolate chip cookies, 33–34,
    234
Christmas traditions, 33–34
and civil rights, 63, 69
clothes, 125, 258
college search, 50–52
confidence, 36, 195
criticism of, 6–7, 235, 237–38,
    242
dating, 40, 99, 100–101
and death of Kennedy, 42
delegation of power by
    husband, 202, 225–26,
    228–29
and disadvantaged minority
    youngsters, 46–47
and Doar, 120–21, 128, 138
driving, 40–41
and education reform, 202,
    204–13
and elective politics, 114, 115
on father, 259
father's illness and death,
    226–27, 243, 253, 254
in Fayetteville (Ark.), 143–45
as First Lady, 243–62
friendships, 39, 65
hair, 150–51
and health care, 19–20, 219,
    226–27, 229, 245, 251–55
in high school, 36, 37–41
and Jones, Don, 17–18, 45,
    47–48, 49–50, 60–61, 62
and King, Martin Luther, 49,
    69–70
on labels, 254–55
as law professor, 137–40
at law school, 77–79, 87–108
as lawyer, 142, 164–70, 173,
    180, 192, 216, 217–18

and legal issues, 140–41,
    145–46, 169–70
maiden name, use of, 170,
    192–93
makeover, 233–34
marriage, 187, 197–98
McGovern campaign, 111–12,
    115–17
meeting of Bill, 100–101
on mother, 259–60
motherhood, 196–97, 261
name change to Clinton,
    193–94
on Nixon, 129, 255, 256
Nixon's criticism of, 4, 7–9,
    10, 20
personal appearance, 5, 39–40,
    55, 150, 194, 233
personality traits, 65–66
political style, 203
as political wife, 149, 156, 171,
    183–85, 194–95, 198, 220
politics, 23–28, 59–60, 63–64
religion, 28–29, 43, 61–63
on Roger Clinton, 215
romance with Bill, 127, 133,
    135, 147–48
on running for office, 216,
    220–21
salary, 164
senior thesis, 77
*60 Minutes* interview, 230–31
speech at University of
    Michigan, 242–43
speech to League of Women
    Voters, 94–95
sports activities, 34, 41
teachers, 37–38
travel, 11
undergraduate years, 55–83
on victory, 11
at victory party, 19
voters' image of, 229
and Watergate affair, 121–27

Clinton, Hillary Rodham (*cont.*)
  wedding, 148–49
  Wellesley commencement
    speech, 59–60, 79–82, 90,
    94, 242
  Wellesley Internship Program,
    72–73
  Wilhelm on, 228
  on women who stay at home,
    229
Clinton, Roger, 214–15
Clinton, Roger, Sr., 215
*The Clintons of Arkansas*, 183,
  184, 191
Coleman, William T. III, 101,
  115
Collier, Harold, 73
Community action programs, 77
Congress, 258
Connally, John, 116–17
Conrad, Larry, 158, 159
*Conscience of a Conservative*, 66
Coulter, Douglas, 157, 159, 161,
  162
Couric, Katie, 255
Cox, Archibald, 119
Cranford, J. Wayne, 190, 195
Cronkite, Walter, 116
Cuban refugees, 182, 188
Cuomo, Mario, 221

Davis, Marlan, 37–38
Davis, Wylie, 136, 137
Day care, 97
Democratic National Convention
  (Chicago), 74–75, 87
Doar, John, 107, 119–24, 126,
  128, 138
Duffey, Joseph D., 99, 114
Dumas, Ernest, 207, 210
Durant, Henry Fowle, 56

Eagleton, Thomas, 115
Eakley, Douglas, 101, 106

Ebeling, Betsy Johnson, 16, 17,
  31, 36, 37, 39, 40, 74, 75
Economy, 221
Edelman, Marian Wright, 90,
  95–98, 118, 216
Edelman, Peter, 90, 216
Education, 95–96, 97, 119,
  201–13, 219
Ehrmann, Sara, 112, 121, 136–37
Emerson, Thomas, 92
Environment, 216
Equal Rights Amendment, 134,
  140, 163, 248
Ethos, 58, 68–69
Executive privilege, 123
Existentialism, 44

Fayetteville (Ark.), 135–37, 140,
  143, 145
FBI, 88, 92
Feulner, Edwin, 74
First Ladies, 7–8, 247–50
Flowers, Gennifer, 18, 185, 187,
  214, 230–31
Ford, Betty, 248
Ford, Gerald, 138, 256
Fortas, Abe, 107
Fort Chaffee (Ark.), 182
Foster, Vincent, Jr., 173
Foster care, 103, 168
Freud, Anna, 98
Fry, Patricia Coffin, 89
Fulbright, J. William, 113

Gaunt, Nancy Hartley, 159
Gearhart, David, 138
Gearhart, Van, 141
Geigreich, William, 158, 159
George, Lloyd, 210
Gephardt, Richard, 221
Giroir, C. Joseph, Jr., 180
Gist, Nancy, 65, 76
Gleckel, Jeffrey, 99–100
Goldstein, Joe, 98

Goldwater, Barry, 23, 25, 26, 27, 66–67
Gore, Al, 18, 19, 221, 234–35
Gore, Tipper, 18, 19, 234–35
Green, Clifford, 61, 232
Greer, Frank, 230
Griffith, Betsy, 64, 76
Grobmyer, Mark, 235
Grove, Lloyd, 35
*Guernica*, 45–46
Guzman, Rafael, 122

Hamilton, Dagmar, 122, 123, 124, 129
Hammerschmidt, John Paul, 114, 127, 135, 145
Hargraves, Ruth, 158, 161
Hart, Gary, 218, 219
Hartke, Vance, 158, 159
*Harvest of Shame*, 97
Health care, 19–20, 219, 226–27, 229, 245, 251–55
Heiden, Sherry, 17, 39
Henry, Ann, 142, 143, 146, 148, 149
Henry, Morris, 148
Hispanics, 47
Holden, Moira, xix
Howell, Della Murray, xviii
Howell, Dorothy *see* Rodham, Dorothy
Howell, Edwin (grandfather), xviii
Howell, Edwin John (great-grandfather), xviii
Howell, Emma Monk, xviii–xix
Howell, Jane Babb, xviii
Hubbell, Webb, 217
Humphrey, Hubert, 63, 74
Hurt, Blant, 212, 213

Impeachment, 121–23, 126, 128–29, 138

Indiana, 156–60, 163
Infant mortality, 219, 237

Jennings, Alston, Sr., 192
Jernigan, William, 220
Johnson, Andrew, 122
Johnson, Lyndon, 8, 23, 24, 26, 27, 28, 67, 74, 89, 117, 241, 256, 257
Johnson, Sid, 210–13
Jones, Don, 17–18, 44–50, 60–63, 69
Jones, Hannah *see* Rodham, Hannah Jones
Jones, Jerry C., 173–74, 190, 191, 194
Jones, Mary Griffiths, xvii
Jones, William, xvi, xvii
Jordan, Hamilton, 157
Jordan, Vernon, 193, 254

Kantor, Mickey, 170
Katz, Jay, 98
Kelley, Virginia Clinton, 10
   on Bill and Hillary, 118, 202, 233
   on husband Roger, 215
   victory party, 15, 16, 19
Kennedy, John F., 42, 241
Kennedy, Robert, 42, 68, 72, 74, 76, 90
Kennedy, William III, 180
Kenney, Charles, 68
Kent State University, 94
Kerrey, Bob, 226
Kesey, Ken, 88
King, Elisabeth, 37
King, Martin Luther, 42, 48–49, 50, 63, 69, 70, 76, 94
King, Patricia, 76
Kirkpatrick, Terry, 122, 124–25, 127–28, 129
Kohler, Otto, 42

Kraft, Tim, 157–58
Kroft, Steve, 186, 231

Laird, Melvin, 72–73
Law Student Civil Rights
    Research Council, 96
League of Women Voters, 90, 94
Legal issues, 140–41, 145–46,
    169–70
Legal Services Corporation
    (LSC), 169, 170, 180, 195, 256
Leverett, Mara, 171
Lindsay, John, 64
Lindsay, Landon, 67
Lindsey, Bruce, 13, 191, 221
Literacy, 237, 248
Little Rock (Ark.), 13–14, 127,
    187, 213
London, Stephen, 57, 67, 69–72
Lugar, Richard, 158
Lyles, Jean, 28

Maraniss, David, 215
Marshall, Burke, 107, 120
Martin, Judith, 82
Martin, Myrna, 150
Mathis, Deborah, 220
Matthews, David, 137, 232–33
Mauro, Gary, 115, 116
McCarthy, Eugene, 15, 67, 74,
    163
McGovern, George, 111–13, 117,
    155, 157, 158, 163
McRae, Tom, 220
Merriwether, James, 165
Methodist church, xvii, 28–29,
    43–44, 67, 197
Meyer-Simon, Diane, 163
Migratory labor, 97
Miller, Mark, 233
Minorities, 138–39
Mondale, Walter, 97, 103–4
Monk, Emma Josephine *see*
    Howell, Emma Monk

Monk, John, xix
Monk, Sarah Abbs, xix
Moore, Frank, 155
Moore, J. William, 88
Moore, Rudy, Jr., 183, 184, 185,
    187, 188, 190
Murdoch, Ellen Press, 24, 27, 28,
    36, 38, 41, 42, 55
Murray, Della *see* Howell, Della
    Murray
Murrow, Edward R., 96–97

National Labor Relations Act, 97
New Hampshire, 67–68
Niebuhr, Reinhold, 44, 62–63
Nixon, Hannah, 7
Nixon, Pat, 7, 248
Nixon, Richard Milhous, 3, 74,
    81, 83, 108, 257
    criticism of Hillary, 4, 7–9, 10,
        20
    Hillary on, 129, 255, 256
    1972 election, 116, 119
    pardon, 138, 256
    relationship with Clintons, 255
    resignation, 129, 256
    Vietnam era, 94
    Watergate, 123, 126, 128, 129,
        135, 256
Nixon, Victor, 148
Nussbaum, Bernard, 121

Osenbaugh, Elizabeth, 139–40

Pappas, Brynda, 159, 160
Parkinson, Ann, xix
Park Ridge (Ill.), 14, 16–17, 25,
    26, 27, 30, 32, 43–44, 46, 78
Perez, Anna, 236
Perot, Margot, 248
Picasso, Pablo, 45
Pinochle, 33
Pogue, Donald, 101, 102, 106
Pollak, Louis S., 89, 92, 93–94

Post, Markie, 233
Poverty, 47
Powell, Jody, 155
Presidential election of 1964, 24, 26–28
Presidential election of 1968, 67, 68, 74
Presidential election of 1972, 111–12, 115, 117
Presidential election of 1988, 218
Presidential election of 1992, 233–38
Protestantism, 61, 63
Pryor, Barbara, 149–51, 172
Pryor, David, 139, 149, 172

Quayle, Dan, 236
Quayle, Marilyn, 235–36

Rape, 142–43
Reagan, Nancy, 248–49
Reagan, Ronald, 182, 195, 248–49
Reed, Julia, 235
Reed, Roy, 191, 202, 206
Reese, Kenneth, 40
Reich, Bob, 102
Religion, 191
Rhodeen, Penn, 102–4, 168
Ricketts, Rick (Ernest), 17, 25, 34, 36, 37, 40, 45, 50
Roberts, Roxanne, 181
Rockefeller, Jeannette, 172
Rockefeller, Nelson, 74
Rockefeller, Winthrop, 172
Rodham, Dorothy, 10, 29, 56
    background, xviii, 32
    on Bill, 106
    and Chelsea, 197
    children, 31, 35–36, 196–97
    Democratic leanings, 25
    and education, 205, 206
    on Hillary, 136
    Hillary on, 259–60

    and Hillary's wedding, 148, 149
    lifestyle, 30, 32
    meeting of Bill, 104–5
Rodham, Elizabeth Scurfield, xix
Rodham, Hannah Jones, xvi–xvii
Rodham, Hugh (brother), 30, 35, 42, 47, 144, 149
Rodham, Hugh (father), 29, 205, 206
    background, 31–32
    brith, xvii
    and Clinton campaign, 144
    as conservative Republican, 25
    Hillary on, 259
    illness, 226–27, 253
    lifestyle, 32
    occupation, 30
    religion, 29
    youth, xvii–xviii
Rodham, Hugh (grandfather), xvi, xvii, 33
Rodham, Isabelle Simpson, xvi, xix
Rodham, Jonathan, xvi, xix
Rodham, Joseph, xix
Rodham, Tony, 30, 31, 35, 39, 144, 149
Rogers, Jeffrey, 102
Rogers, Kristine Olson, 60, 69, 88, 89, 92–93, 102, 106, 115
Roosevelt, Eleanor, 247
Roosevelt, Teddy, 7
Rose law firm, 165–66, 172, 173, 179–82, 192, 214, 216, 218
Rostow, Eugene, 89
Rule, Herb, 165
Rutherford, Skip, 12–13, 204

Salinger, J. D., 45
Santmire, H. Paul, 61
Schechter, Alan, 66, 68, 72, 77, 78–79
Scheibner, Nancy, 81
Schlafly, Phyllis, 134

Schools *see* Education
Schreiber, William, 160, 161
Schweitzer, Albert, 254
Scranton (Pa.), xvi, xix
Seale, Bobby, 87, 91, 93
Sexual revolution, 66
Shapiro, Constance Hoenk, 60
Sheehy, Gail, 101, 190, 233
Sherrill, Martha, 31, 37, 56
Shields, Geoffrey, 64
*60 Minutes*, 186, 230–31
Smith, Craig, 13, 221
Smith, Margaret Chase, 115
Smith, Stephen A., 184–85
Smith College, 50, 51
Socks (cat), 4
Solnit, Al, 98
Soviet Union, 221
Spragens, Janet Altman, 50–51
Steenburgen, Mary, 233
Stein, Sidney H., 106
Student Nonviolent Coordinating
    Committee, 63
Supreme Court, 66

Taxes, 162, 209–11
Teacher competency, 207–12
Texas, 116–17, 157
Thomases, Susan, 193
Tillich, Paul, 48

University of Arkansas, 135, 137
University of Life, 44, 50
University of Michigan, 242

Vaught, Worley Oscar, 191
Verveer, Melanie, 253
Vida Dutton Scudder Fellowship,
    89
Vietnam War, 8, 59, 67, 73, 74,
    76, 81, 87, 113, 116, 236, 256
Volner, Jill Wine, 124
Voting, of 18-year-olds, 90, 112,
    115

Wang, Kwan Kwan, 97, 98, 100
Watergate affair, 111, 113, 116,
    117, 119, 121–27, 128–29, 256
Watters, Susan, 233–34
Weicker, Lowell, 99
Weld, Bill, 123, 124
Wellesley College, 50–52, 55–59,
    64, 68, 71, 75, 76, 83
Wesley, John, xvii, 29, 180
White, Frank, 188–89, 217
Wilhelm, David, 12, 228, 230,
    231, 237
Wills, Garry, 118
Wilson, Francine Rusan, 58, 59,
    64, 65, 71, 83
Wilson, William R., Jr., 165,
    166–67
Women
    in Arkansas, 127, 141, 146
    elective offices for, 115
    for Hillary, 10
    lawyers, 141, 165, 168
    Nixon's views, 7, 9
    opportunities for, 70–71, 261
    in political jobs, 163
    role of, 11
    stay-at-home, 229
    at University of Arkansas,
        138–39
    working, 9
    at Yale, 88–89
    *see also* Equal Rights
    Amendment; Rape
Woods, Harriet, 228, 234
Woodward, Bob, 116
Woodward, Judith, 16
Wright, Betsey, 112–13, 156–57,
    189–90, 192, 193, 207–210,
    214, 215, 229
Wright, Lindsey & Jennings, 191

Yale Law School, 77–79, 87–94,
    107, 145
Yates, Pauline, 41